Contents

DISC-BASED LEADERSHIP

A Leader's Guide to Team Effectiveness

Empowered Leadership. Trust Building. Healthy Communication. Conflict Management. Effective Meetings. DISC Interviewing. People Reading. Facilitated Team Activities.

For permission requests,
write to the author at the address below.
Leadership Alive, Inc. | PO Box 69652 | Tucson, AZ 85737

ISBN: 979-8-9886661-8-9 (paperback)
ISBN: 979-8-9887643-9-7 (hardback)
ISBN: 978-1-64316-182-2 (ebook)

LeadershipAlive.com
Chris@LeadershipAlive.com

Printed in the United States of America
Author: Christopher P. Meade, PhD
Cover design by Kevin Piazza
Editing: Rob Peace, David Elmore and Allison Meade

1.
Empowered Leadership: Harnessing DISC for Team Success

Empowered leadership is like a kaleidoscope, where the colors of Dominance, Influence, Steadiness, and Conscientiousness converge to create an intricate, harmonious pattern of success.
— Christopher Meade, PhD

Are you ready to be the leader you've always thought you could be? Just in case there was any doubt: you *are*. So let's take a journey. As you venture into this book, you'll embark upon a voyage of discovery, growth, and leadership excellence. The DISC framework will help you understand how you approach the world and offer you the necessary tools to lead more effectively. You'll learn to manage with empathy, foster a team culture that thrives on diversity, and, most importantly, generate exceptional results.

We know that leadership style varies, correct? It depends on the individual, on their personality, and on what history, knowledge, and traits they bring to the table. Acknowledging this is the first step toward success. We're going to identify, categorize, and flesh out those styles to make you a greater leader.

As you delve into the various distinctive DISC leadership styles, you'll gain valuable insight into your approach, including your unique strengths. Whether you embody the D (Dominance) style, I (Influence) style, S (Steadiness) style, or C (Conscientiousness) style, you'll discover new ways to leverage your innate strengths and manage weaknesses (yes, we all have a few of those). Equipped with this knowledge, you'll better understand your colleagues, superiors, and subordinates and more capably drive effective communication and collaboration.

The DISC framework is an invaluable template for anyone in management. Beyond helping you manage tasks and processes, it delves into the heart of one of your most critical duties—managing people. Understanding that each team member has their own behavioral and communication style empowers you, as a leader, to resonate with them. With the DISC lens in hand, you'll motivate and engage your colleagues in a manner that aligns with their unique outlook and approach.

The DISC framework illustrates the diverse ways people view and interact with the world. Recognizing and harnessing the power of diversity leads to a more harmonious, creative, and dynamic work environment, transforming individual pursuits into cohesive teamwork—where everyone's strengths are valued and leveraged, and weaknesses are understood and mitigated.

But this book isn't just a guide—it's a journey into understanding people, beginning with *you*. Through the lens of the DISC framework, you'll learn how to lead with empathy, manage with understanding, and create a team culture that thrives on diversity and unity.

DISC Influences How We See the World

Your unique behavioral pattern and communication style profoundly influence how you perceive the world and those around you. With this in mind (how you're influenced), the DISC framework helps you better understand your behavioral tendencies, improving all your interactions—both personal and professional.

Imagine your behavioral style as a set of lenses through which you interpret your experiences. You don't perceive things as *they* are—you perceive them as *you* are. This isn't necessarily bad; it's simply human nature. Your DISC profile—whether Dominance, Influence, Steadiness, or Conscientiousness—shapes your view of the world. None of these styles is intrinsically superior or inferior to another. They're just different ways of seeing, processing, and communicating with the world around you.

For instance, if you're primarily a D-style individual, you might see the world as a competitive arena where results are everything. You might adopt a direct, assertive communication style, expecting others to mirror your approach. In a team setting where project deadlines are tight, your D-style lens might drive you to push for efficiency and results first, with team harmony being a distant second—if it's even on your radar at all.

An I-style individual might view the world as a stage filled with excitement and endless opportunities. You're probably an enthusiastic and friendly person, always keen to build and nurture relationships. You might thrive on engaging others with your creative and infectious energy in brainstorming sessions. You probably see ideas as thrilling opportunities rather than challenges.

The S-style person usually cherishes stability, predictability, and harmony in their work environment. A leader working with this type of team member might tailor their communication style toward providing them with the consistency and support they need to feel engaged and comfortable within their responsibilities.

Finally, if you lean toward a C-style, you likely interpret the world through a lens of order, structure, and logic. You highly value accuracy, precision, and careful analysis. During a project planning phase, you meticulously analyze every detail and demand accuracy, seeing these as crucial to a project's success.

This DISC framework, once understood, offers a practical way of understanding and leveraging diverse human behavior and communication styles. By grasping and implementing it, you'll appreciate the uniqueness of others and learn how to harness their abilities to enhance collaboration and optimize interactions.

DISC Creates a More Inclusive Workplace

Implementing the DISC lens within your team promotes an inclusive workplace. Equipping yourself and colleagues with a better understanding of diverse communication and work styles enhances collaboration and celebrates diversity.

If you're a D-style leader, you're probably direct and task-oriented (nose to the grindstone). This can be quite productive but often lacks a certain vitality (the input of others). So then, expand your leadership effectiveness by valuing the perspectives and contributions of team members who thrive in a collaborative environment and have a keen eye for detail. Acknowledging others will cultivate a sense of belonging and inclusivity among colleagues—and achieve even greater results.

If you're an I-style team member, you bring unmatched energy and enthusiasm to work. Good on you! But while your lively spirit is valuable, you can further contribute to an inclusive environment by recognizing and appreciating input from those who are reserved and analytical. This balanced dynamic inspires an atmosphere of mutual respect and understanding.

As an S-style team member, you highly value harmony and collaboration (vital qualities in all workplaces). But fostering an inclusive space often involves assertively advocating for your needs when necessary, striking the right balance between maintaining peace and ensuring your voice is heard.

Or as a C-style team member, you're known throughout the company for meticulous attention to accuracy and precision (the "go-to" person). While these traits are essential, creating an inclusive environment might involve being flexible and adaptable to change, thereby demonstrating an openness to varying methods and approaches, which results in an inclusive workplace.

By leveraging the DISC model, you deepen your understanding and appreciation of your team's diverse communication and work styles. When team members feel understood and valued for their uniqueness, there's a greater sense of mutual respect and appreciation, which makes the workplace genuinely inclusive.

DISC Leadership Styles

The DISC assessment gives you valuable insight into your leadership style and a deeper understanding of how your behaviors influence others. Each DISC style—Dominance, Influence, Steadiness, and Conscientiousness—has its unique characteristics and strengths, which, when used effectively, create a powerful leadership dynamic.

If you have a formidable Dominance (D) style, your strength lies in your direct, decisive, and results-oriented nature. You're seen as a confident risk taker who always focuses on the big picture. But perhaps it's not always the *entire* picture. Imagine a situation where your team needs to pivot rapidly due to market changes. Your ability to alter course and make quick, decisive decisions in that regard will guide your team successfully through the changes.

If you're a leader with the Influence (I) style, there's a good chance you're seen as outgoing, optimistic, and socially skilled. You excel at networking, relationship building, and persuasive communication. Let your charisma shine when inspiring your team during company-wide meetings or by bringing stakeholders on board for new projects.

Or you may have the Steadiness (S) style of leadership. You're known for your supportive, loyal, and patient demeanor, and you're often seen as a team player and active listener. You're detail-oriented and you place a high value on stability and harmony. This strength might come into play when mediating a conflict between team members, where your supportive nature restores balance.

If you're a leader with a style high in Conscientiousness (C), you're analytical, logical, and precise. Known for being systematic and organized, you're driven by data and facts, striving for accuracy and efficiency. Your skills prove invaluable when your team is tackling a complex project that requires detailed planning and problem solving.

Summary

You'll maximize your potential as a leader by understanding (and conscientiously using) the unique strengths and characteristics of the four DISC leadership styles. Embracing the differences and recognizing the strengths of each style will help you form a more cohesive and successful team dynamic.

And it isn't simply about understanding how *you* lead but also understanding that *others* may lead differently. Recognizing different leadership styles within your team helps promote a culture of respect and appreciation for diversity of thought and action.

Moving into the next chapter, you'll discover how each DISC style significantly shapes a harmonious and productive work environment.

Team Discussion Questions

1. How have you noticed your DISC leadership style influencing your interactions and decision-making process? Can you share a specific example of a time when your style was particularly evident?

2. In what way can the DISC framework help you improve team collaboration and communication? Share a scenario of when understanding different styles could've led to more effective collaboration.

3. Identify a time when understanding a colleague's DISC style could've helped you improve an outcome or communicate better. How could you use this awareness in future situations?

4. How does your DISC style contribute to your team's diversity and success? How can you leverage your unique strengths and insight in upcoming projects?

5. How can we use our understanding of DISC to create a more inclusive and empathetic team culture? Can you propose some actionable steps that would enhance your appreciation for the unique styles of others and garner a more inclusive environment?

2.
DISC Leadership Styles: The Four Strengths

Dominance navigates the storm, Influence ignites the spark, Steadiness anchors the ship, and Conscientiousness charts the course. Together, they form the compass of diverse leadership.
— Christopher Meade, PhD

Let's delve into the quintessential strengths woven into each DISC leadership style. By understanding them, you'll bolster your leadership capabilities and learn to appreciate those of your team members.

1. **Dominance (D) leadership style.** As a D-style leader, your decisiveness guides your team through pressing challenges. Your willpower and confidence are the backbone of your leadership, allowing you to stand committed to a clear vision and remain intensely results-driven—even in a situation that requires you to navigate your team through a sudden market downturn. Here, your natural ability to make swift, calculated decisions presents itself, enabling your team to adapt and strive for desired outcomes.

2. **Influence (I) leadership style.** As an I-style leader, your charisma shines brightly as you motivate your team and inspire them to reach new heights. Your exceptional communication skills are akin to a harmonious orchestra. You ensure that each team member feels heard and understood, and that they remain integral to the team's journey. You effortlessly bring an optimistic spirit to work, spark en-

thusiasm, and create a buzzing atmosphere. When tasked with a new project, your infectious optimism and engaging communication style inspire your team, making daunting projects seem exciting.

3. **Steadiness (S) leadership style.** With an S-style leadership, your deep-seated loyalty and commitment make a palpable difference to team efforts. Like a tranquil lake, your patience assures that you handle pressure with grace and resilience. Your keen attention to detail makes you an excellent organizer. You ensure that all of your team's moving parts fire in perfect unison. On a high-pressure deadline, you remain calm and organized, guaranteeing that your team meets challenges head-on with little stress.

4. **Conscientiousness (C) leadership style.** As a C-style leader, your analytic and systematic approach carves a smooth pathway through the most complex problems. You set a high bar for quality and precision, and you ensure that your team consistently delivers exceptional results. When tackling a complex project with multiple variables, your detail-oriented mindset leads you to create a comprehensive plan, dissecting the task into manageable parts and maintaining a strong focus on quality control.

The vibrant tapestry of your leadership style becomes apparent when you gain a firm grasp on these strengths. Effective leadership often requires a blend of different strengths and styles. Understanding your DISC style helps you capitalize on your strengths and effectively manage your limitations.

The Overuse of DISC Strengths

A DISC leadership style is of little use if we don't know its unique strengths and potential weaknesses. In fact, the style could even be counterproductive. An overused strength can become a weakness. For example, even though you may be quite good with team members, you may not be reading the "people context" accurately. This can lead to misunderstanding, misinterpretation, or conflict among your team. Recognizing these potential pitfalls will help you communicate more effectively, collaborate better, and boost overall team performance. Many "misunderstandings" are caused by the overuse of one's particular DISC strength with someone else who has a different DISC style. Let's dive a bit further into the idea of overuse.

If you're a D-style leader, you may come across as overly aggressive or domineering. Being results-focused, you might overlook the importance of building and nurturing relationships. For example, during team meetings, your direct and assertive approach may unintentionally shut down others' opinions. Though your dominance and confidence drive progress and inspire action, it's essential to improve your listening skills and consider the perspectives of others.

With I-style leadership, you may prioritize popularity over productivity. You might experience challenges related to organization and follow-through, as well as to making tough decisions. Although your charismatic and enthusiastic personality shines during brainstorming sessions, you may need help bringing creative ideas to fruition due to weak follow-through. Though your communication skills and ability to inspire others are powerful, it's crucial to pay attention to details and execute plans efficiently.

As an S-style leader, you may be seen as risk-averse, indecisive, and overly focused on maintaining harmony—sometimes at the expense of achieving results. For example, you might find it challenging to implement necessary changes due to fear of disrupting team harmony. While your supportive nature fosters solid relationships and collaboration, becoming more assertive and willing to embrace change will help you be a more effective leader.

Finally, the delegation of duties and effective communication might pose challenges if you resonate with the C-style leadership. You may be perceived as overly critical or a perfectionist, prioritizing data over people. In team projects, you struggle to delegate tasks due to your high standards and "obsession" with precision. Although your analytical skills and fixation on quality are assets, developing flexibility and understanding the value of team collaboration will enhance leadership effectiveness.

Summary

As we reflect on these leadership styles, their strengths, and their potential pitfalls (overuse), we should remember that these are broad tendencies, not definitive rules. Every individual is unique. While some may exhibit traits closely aligned with their DISC leadership style, others may embody a blend of styles. Making a deliberate effort to understand these nuances helps you grow as a leader and encourage a sense of inclusivity and respect within your team.

This awareness is vital. By recognizing potential weaknesses, you become more equipped to address them proactively, refining your leadership style, building a harmonious team dynamic, and increasing overall productivity. Your strengths and limitations are learning opportunities to become a more versatile, compassionate, and effective leader.

In the next chapter, we'll explore how to boost team trust using DISC, including unlocking team potential through greater understanding, acceptance, and respect.

Team Discussion Questions

1. Which of the four DISC leadership styles do you resonate with the most? Can you identify a recent situation where you

demonstrated some strengths typical of this style? How did it impact your team and the outcome?

2. Every leadership style features strengths and weaknesses, and it's common to overuse our strengths. Can you identify a time when you overused your DISC strength? How did it affect the situation? How might you approach things differently next time?

3. In what way do various DISC leadership styles manifest in your team? How do different styles complement one another, and where do they cause conflict?

4. Given your understanding of your leadership style, what steps can you take to balance your strengths and weaknesses and prevent your strengths from becoming overused?

5. Considering the potential limitations of your DISC leadership style, what specific actions can you take to mitigate them and become a more well-rounded leader? How might you help others in your team do the same?

3.
Boosting Team Trust

Harmony in a team begins with a melody of trust,
and DISC is the tuning fork that brings our diverse
notes into perfect pitch.

— Christopher Meade, PhD

Embracing DISC dramatically amplifies trust within your team, creating strong bonds and an environment rooted in understanding and respect. The first step to building this foundation lies in shared language and comprehension among team members. The powerful DISC tool allows teams to decrypt their unique communication and behavioral styles, recognizing and appreciating each other's strengths and navigate potential challenges.

Let's say a project manager has a Dominance (D) style. With a new understanding of the DISC framework, what was once considered an overly assertive and intimidating approach is now revered as a powerful drive that gets results.

Consider a team member with a Steadiness (S) style—they have a calm demeanor and a preference for consistency and stability. Before understanding DISC, other members might've mistaken their focus on routine as resistance to change. With the application of DISC, this approach is now seen as a valuable trait that inspires stability and reliability. This shared understanding helps members anticipate and adapt to each other's needs, cultivating a sense of trust and camaraderie.

Cultivating Self-Awareness

Another element of trust building with DISC is nurturing self-awareness. Understanding your DISC profile helps you understand your unique communication style. This heightened self-awareness guides you to communicate more genuinely and aids in the creation of a transparent and trust-filled team environment.

Say you're a leader with an Influence (I) style. Upon recognizing your natural tendency to be enthusiastic and expressive, you might know (or come to learn) that you occasionally struggle with detailed tasks. This awareness enables you to approach your work more thoughtfully, ensuring that your actions align with team expectations, thus fortifying trust.

Suppose you identify with a Conscientiousness (C) style. Recognizing your inherent tendency for precision and meticulousness, you know that you occasionally struggle with rapid decision making. This awareness inspires you to communicate your need for thorough examination and discussion before making important decisions. It helps align your actions with team expectations, thereby reinforcing trust.

Healthy Communication

DISC helps us refine communication and conflict-resolution skills within team settings. Once you fully grasp the individual communication styles of team members, you can express your needs and perspectives more effectively, and vice versa. By understanding each other's conflict-resolution styles, you can prevent potential misunderstandings and manage conflict more efficiently to avoid diminished trust.

Most importantly, DISC cultivates a team culture drenched in empathy and respect. These virtues blossom from understanding and cherishing the diversity of communication and behavioral styles—a culture of deep-seated trust where each member feels valued, safe, and supported.

Decoding Each Other's DISC Styles

Imagine a marketing team often entangled by trust issues. By applying DISC training, team members quickly begin to decode each other's unique styles. This newfound understanding ignites an appreciation for individual strengths and weaknesses, leading to more sincere and improved communication. By mastering conflict resolution, you avoid misunderstandings and disagreements to solidify trust further. Over time, your team's culture gradually transforms into a hub of empathy and respect, further cementing trust and cohesion.

By comprehending and decoding with the principles of DISC, you'll lay down the cornerstone for trust within teams—an essential ingredient for success. These principles help refine communication, infuse empathy, nurture productive collaboration, and boost accountability, laying a roadmap for successful conflict resolution.

Trust-Building Elements

Improved communication is yet another of the primary benefits of understanding DISC. By acknowledging the unique communication styles of team members, you tailor your communication style to align with each individual. For example, a Dominance (D) style teammate will appreciate brevity and clarity, while an Influence (I) style individual will resonate with a more enthusiastic, personal interaction.

Empathy, the ability to understand and share the feelings of others, is another vital component in trust building that DISC facilitates. When you recognize the unique DISC styles of teammates, you can better understand their perspectives and motivations, which engenders empathy, smoother interactions, and bond-building within teams.

With a comprehensive understanding of DISC, you allocate tasks by team member style to encourage respect and trust. For instance, a Steadiness (S) team member may excel in a role that values consistency and support, while a Conscientiousness (C) individual might thrive at detail-oriented tasks requiring meticulous analysis.

Accountability is another fundamental aspect of trust. When team members understand their DISC styles and associated expectations, they hold themselves more accountable.

Finally, DISC arms you with the skills necessary to successfully navigate conflict resolution. By understanding team members' unique conflict-resolution styles, you can address disputes respectfully and constructively, avoiding misunderstandings that chip away at trust.

The interplay of these factors—improved communication, increased empathy, effective collaboration, amplified accountability, and successful conflict resolution—elicits highly cohesive and productive teams. A team bound by trust and mutual respect is a team that achieves shared goals and reaches new heights of success.

Tips to Build Trust With the Four Styles

Each of the four DISC styles entails distinct preferences, facilitating a strong sense of trust within teams when acknowledged and catered to. The following is a handy guide, including a few tips, to build trust tailored to each style:

1. **For Dominance (D) teammates.** These individuals value forthrightness, confidence, and a results-oriented approach. To establish trust with D-style colleagues, practice directness and transparency in your communication. Exhibit confidence in your capabilities. Consistently show

that you're driven by results. Imagine you're collaborating on a project with a D-style teammate. You present proposals backed by data and evidence. You're prepared to argue your stance with rationality and cogency, and to demonstrate confidence and commitment to achieving results.

You're speaking their language by presenting proposals backed by data and evidence, showing that you respect their time by being prepared and direct. This is precisely what D-style individuals want to see: clear, straightforward, and rational arguments with evident focus on end goals and results.

Here's what might be going on inside a D-style individual's head during such an interaction:

They're clear and direct in their communication, not wasting any time. They're prepared and confident, presenting their proposals with concrete data and evidence, just as I like it, and they're even ready to debate their stance rationally. This shows me they're as competent and results-driven as I am. I appreciate this straightforward, no-nonsense approach. I can trust this person because they demonstrate a strong commitment to achieving results, just like I do.

By aligning yourself with the D-style individual's preference for efficiency, directness, and results-oriented thinking, you show that you understand and respect their viewpoints. Mutual understanding and respect are paramount for building trust with D-style individuals.

2. **For Influence (I) teammates.** These cohorts treasure relationships, cooperative work, and a touch of fun. To cultivate trust with your I-style colleagues, display a genuine interest in their ideas. Be ready to brainstorm and collaborate. Introduce a bit of humor and positivity into your interactions. Suppose you pair with an I-style team member

on a project. Welcome their suggestions and actively listen to their input. With these types, a little bit of lightheartedness goes a long way.

Building trust with an I-style individual is about appreciating and supporting their strengths and adjusting your behavior to their style. Not only should you listen to their ideas but also validate them. Engage in a bit of back-and-forth to refine ideas. Some well-placed humor and positive vibes are crucial. This not only makes them feel comfortable but also valued.

Here's what might be going on in an I-style person's head during a positive interaction:

Wow, they really value my ideas and input. We're bouncing off each other and coming up with some clever solutions. Plus, the conversation is fun and positive, so I feel comfortable sharing my creative thoughts without fear of being shot down or judged negatively. I trust this person because they show me respect and appreciate my perspectives. They make the process enjoyable.

Ensuring that I-style individuals feel understood, appreciated, and valued for their unique way of thinking builds trust. By aligning with their style, you demonstrate empathy, understanding, and a willingness to meet them halfway—all critical components of trust.

3. **For Steadiness (S) teammates.** S-styles appreciate stability, predictability, and harmonious environments. To nurture confidence with them, prove yourself reliable, consistent, and supportive. Show that you value their viewpoints, and work to create a harmonious and cooperative atmosphere. For instance, if you're working alongside an S-style team member, ensure that you're fulfilling your commitments to the best of your ability. Show patience and understanding for their preference for a stable and predictable work envi-

ronment. Do this, and you'll show them that you respect them.

Here's what could be going on in an S-style individual's head during such an interaction:

This person consistently fulfills their commitments and respects my need for a stable and predictable work environment. They're patient and understanding, and they don't rush things or push for abrupt changes. This is exactly the kind of work environment I thrive in. I feel heard and valued. This makes it easy for me to express my thoughts and ideas. I trust this person because they're reliable and respectful of my preferences.

By aligning your actions with the values and preferences of S-style individuals, you demonstrate respect and understanding, effectively building trust.

4. **For Conscientiousness (C) teammates.** These individuals value meticulousness, precision, and thoroughness. To establish trust with your C-style teammates, exhibit a meticulous and detail-oriented approach. Provide clear and concise instruction, remain well-prepared and organized, and show that you've thoroughly considered all aspects and potential outcomes of a project.

   When you exhibit thoroughness and a detail-oriented approach, you communicate effectively in their preferred style. You show that you understand and respect how they work, demonstrating an understanding of their core values and proving that you're willing to align your approach with theirs.

   Here's a look into what a C-style individual may be thinking during such an interaction:

   This person is thorough and seems to appreciate the tiny details as much as I do. They've taken the time to provide clear and concise instructions, and they've thought about all the possible outcomes. This tells me that they value preparation and organization, just like I do. I feel understood and respected, and I trust this person because they approach work the same way I do. I don't have to worry about ambiguity or disorganization. I can be confident that they consider all aspects before making decisions.

Building trust with a C-style individual in this way shows that you value the same things they do—meticulousness, thoroughness, and precision. If they feel that you're consistently organized and detail-oriented, they'll be more comfortable working with you on shared tasks and projects.

Summary

Building trust is a powerful yet delicate process, consciously tailored for each individual. It involves a keen understanding of each team member's DISC style and a willingness to adjust and adapt your actions to align with their unique preferences. By observing, understanding, and aligning with each DISC style's individual preferences and values, you don't just build trust—you also pave the way for a more harmonious and productive work environment. With trust as a foundational pillar, you position your team to conquer any challenge that comes its way, bolstering performance, engagement, and success.

In the next chapter, prepare to unlock the secrets of leveraging the DISC model to hone your persuasive prowess, build deep connections, and influence others effectively across countless interpersonal scenarios.

Team Discussion Questions

1. Reflecting on your DISC leadership style, what steps can you take to strengthen trust within your team?

2. How does understanding each team member's DISC style improve communication and prevent misunderstanding? Can you share an instance when this understanding could've been beneficial?

3. Discuss a situation where you've recognized and appreciated a colleague's strengths, including how this awareness impacted your relationship and collaboration efforts. What did you learn from this experience?

4. Self-awareness is a crucial aspect of fostering trust within teams. How has your understanding of your DISC profile helped you communicate more genuinely and align your actions with team expectations?

5. In terms of conflict resolution, how does understanding each other's DISC style help you manage disagreements more efficiently and preserve trust? Can you provide an example of a situation where this understanding could've made a significant difference?

4.
The Art of Persuasion: Navigating With DISC

The DISC persuasion approach is like learning every individual's unique dance. When you know the steps, you lead gracefully, harmoniously influencing the ballroom of interactions.

— Christopher Meade, PhD

"The key to successful influence is leadership, not authority," said Ken Blanchard, American author and business pro. It's definitely true, and the ability to influence and persuade others isn't just a skill—it's a potent catalyst that propels us forward through the maelstrom of life, from boardroom negotiations to dinner table conversations and everything in between. Be it in the world of business, the corridors of politics, or the intimate sphere of personal relationships, persuasive communication is an art that forms the bedrock of successful interactions.

Persuasion isn't about strong-arming someone into agreement (that "toxic authority" thing we all know and loathe); rather, we must connect with their unique needs, desires, and preferences. It's about crafting a message that vibrates on their wavelength, truly resonates, and kindles a harmonious response. We talk in the listener's language, echoing their intrinsic motivations and perspectives. This is where true persuasive power lies.

A Gateway to Effective Persuasion

The DISC model serves as a trusty compass to guide you in interpersonal understanding. Named for the four primary behavioral traits it identifies—Dominance (D), Influence (I), Steadiness (S), and Conscientiousness (C)—this model navigates the diverse landscape of human communication and decision-making styles. It paints a detailed picture of how people process information, react to situations, and make choices.

By leveraging the insights of the DISC model, you'll understand the varied lenses through which others view the world, enabling you to tailor your communication strategies and adjust your style to deliver a message that truly connects. It's the key that unlocks the door to more profound empathy, improved rapport, and enhanced persuasion. As you navigate the terrain of influence and persuasion, let the DISC framework be your trusty and effective guide.

Below are some tips for becoming more persuasive by using each of the four DISC styles.

1. **Persuading a D-style colleague.** Being direct, concise, and results-oriented is essential when working with a D-style person. They want clear evidence that your ideas or proposals will lead to tangible benefits and outcomes. Use data and facts to support your arguments. For instance, if you pitch a new sales strategy to a D-style manager, come armed with data highlighting how this approach has improved sales in other organizations. Be prepared to defend your position if challenged, and avoid getting bogged down in details or hypothetical scenarios.

   When it comes to persuasion, D-style individuals appreciate a straightforward approach emphasizing clear benefits and tangible outcomes. Using data and facts gives them an objective basis for decision making and resonates with their results-driven nature.

Here's what might be going on in the mind of a D-style individual during a persuasive exchange (if you lean into their preferred style):

This person is presenting their idea with clear, tangible results. They're not wasting time on unnecessary details or hypotheticals but are focusing on concrete evidence that supports the benefits of their proposal. They're confident, which tells me that they believe in their proposal and are prepared to stand by it. They're giving me the bottom line without the fluff. This appeals to me because I want to see results, and they're showing me how we can get them. This directness and clarity make it easier for me to trust in the proposal and the person presenting it.

A straightforward, results-oriented approach persuades the D-style individual because it aligns with their desire for efficiency and tangible outcomes. They don't want to sift through extraneous information to get to the point. They value actions over words and results over processes. When you communicate directly, focus on results, and use concrete evidence, you show D-style people that you understand and align with their core values, making your message more persuasive.

2. **Persuading an I-style colleague.** I-style people respond well to enthusiastic, upbeat messages that appeal to their sense of fun and excitement. Use storytelling and anecdotes to illustrate the benefits of your idea or proposals. For example, if you suggest a team-building event to an I-style colleague, use an engaging story from a similar past event that highlights the camaraderie it created. Emphasize the social or emotional impact it'll have. Use humor and positivity to keep the mood light and engaging.

When it comes to persuasion, I-style individuals respond best to a lively, animated approach. They appreciate storytelling and anecdotes to add a personal and emotional dimension to the discussion. They're primarily interested in the relational and social impacts of decisions and actions rather than facts and figures.

During a persuasive conversation (if you lean into their preferred style), an I-style individual might be thinking:

This person is speaking my language! They use engaging stories and anecdotes to make their ideas more relatable and real. I can imagine myself in these scenarios, and they sound like a lot of fun. I feel more connected to their proposal because it resonates with me emotionally and socially. It's not just about achieving a target or a goal—it's also about enjoying the journey and enhancing relationships. They're keeping the conversation light and positive. This appeals to my optimistic nature.

This approach persuades the I-style individual because it aligns with their preference for energetic, collaborative, and enthusiastic interactions. You meet I-style people in their comfort zone with anecdotes, humor, and positivity—making them feel understood and connected to your ideas and making your message more persuasive.

3. **Persuading an S-style colleague.** S-style people value stability, security, and relationships. When trying to convince them, focus on long-term benefits. For instance, if proposing a change in a work process, stress how it will lead to a more consistent and stable workflow. Emphasize how it'll help build trust and strengthen relationships, and take the time to listen to their concerns. Address any fears or uncertainties they have, and use a collaborative, cooperative approach that emphasizes teamwork and mutual benefits.

When it comes to persuasion, S-style people respond best to approaches prioritizing stability, continuity, and mutual support. They appreciate knowing that change will enhance their secure, predictable environment and strengthen their relationships rather than cause unnecessary disruption or chaos.

When you approach an S-style person with a persuasive argument in their preferred style, they might be thinking:

This person understands that I value stability and long-term benefits. They're not trying to rush me into a decision. They're considering how the change will improve our workflow and lead to stronger relationships. I appreciate that they take the time to listen to my concerns and are willing to address them. Their cooperative and team-oriented approach makes me feel supported and more at ease with the proposed change.

This approach persuades the S-style person by reassuring them that their need for stability and security is acknowledged and respected. By focusing on long-term benefits and demonstrating an understanding of their concerns, you show them that you've considered the impact of your proposal on their comfort and stability. This aligns with their values and makes your message more persuasive.

4. **Persuading a C-style colleague.** C-style people are analytical and detail-oriented. They value accuracy, precision, and logic. When persuading them, be prepared with data, research, and evidence to support your argument. If you suggest new software to a C-style team member, use data and analysis to prove how it has helped other teams. Emphasize the practical benefits and measurable outcomes of your ideas or proposals. Be prepared to answer tough questions and objections, and use a logical, structured approach that follows a step-by-step process.

In the context of persuasion, you sway C-style people with well-researched, logically sound arguments supported by evidence. They want to see that you've done your homework and that the changes you're proposing aren't just whims but are backed up by credible data, thorough research, and logical reasoning.

When you approach a C-style person with a persuasive argument in their preferred style, they might be thinking:

This person has taken time to do extensive research. They're not making assumptions or jumping to conclusions—they're presenting detailed evidence with clear, logical reasoning. Their proposal aligns with the practical, measurable outcomes that I value. They're prepared to answer challenging questions and can explain how we'll get from point A to point B.

C-style people find this approach persuasive because it meets their need for thoroughness, precision, and logic. It demonstrates that you've considered all aspects of your proposal and are prepared to defend it based on evidence, not just rhetoric and persuasion. You build trust and credibility by respecting their need for details, data, and logical processes, making your arguments more persuasive.

The Path to Mastering Persuasion

In your journey to master the art of persuasion and influence, understanding and using the four DISC styles serve as an invaluable tool. The key lies not in molding others to fit your style but in tailoring your communication style to resonate with theirs.

If you're dealing with a Dominance (D) individual, be direct, results-oriented, and back your ideas with data. With Influence (I) teammates, harness the power of enthusiasm, storytelling, and the human touch to spark excitement. For Steadiness (S) people, highlight your proposals' stable, long-term benefits. When it comes to Conscientiousness (C) people, use precision, logical reasoning, and meticulously researched evidence to pave the way.

Adapting your style to suit others isn't insincere or manipulative. Quite to the contrary—it confidently bridges gaps, creates connections, and establishes meaningful communication. Each DISC style comes with its own set of unique strengths and perspectives. By embracing these differences, not only will you empower yourself to be more persuasive but you'll also create an environment of mutual respect and understanding. So gear up and put these insights into practice to begin navigating diverse DISC landscapes gracefully and effortlessly.

As we progress into the next chapter, you'll discover how you can use the DISC model to transform your approach to conflict management, enabling you to turn potential roadblocks into powerful opportunities for growth and understanding.

Team Discussion Questions

1. How would you categorize your primary style based on your understanding of the DISC model? How does it influence your communication style in the workplace? Can you share an example of a time when your style benefited or hindered a workplace interaction?

2. Can you recall a time when you tailored your communication style to match another team member's DISC style? How did you adapt, and what was the outcome?

3. How can your team apply the principles of the DISC model to improve daily interactions and overall team performance? Are there any specific strategies that would be particularly beneficial?

4. How might understanding and accommodating the various DISC styles help you cultivate an environment of mutual respect and understanding within your team?

5. Reflect on a time when you successfully persuaded a colleague or superior using strategies aligned with their DISC style. What methods did you use, and why do you think they were effective?

5.
Conflict Management:
The DISC Approach

Applying DISC to conflict resolution is like turning on a flashlight in a dark room. It illuminates unique perspectives, guiding you toward a solution that promotes unity and turns conflict into a stepping stone for growth and innovation.

— Christopher Meade, PhD

Conflict is inevitable—we all know that. But it's also eminently manageable. Not everyone knows that or, especially, *how* to do that. Navigating the choppy waters of conflict within your team or organization can be daunting, but it's a reality you must face. Tackling it with the right tools and strategies will strengthen relationships and create a more harmonious work environment. By leveraging the insights of the DISC framework in communication styles, preferences, and behavioral patterns, you can build more effective strategies for conflict resolution.

The beauty of the DISC approach lies in its ability to highlight the unique ways we process information, respond to stress, and interact with others. By understanding these nuances, you address conflict with a respect and appreciation for these differences rather than brushing them aside. Conflict isn't always a sign of dysfunction— sometimes it's simply an organic part of the business process, with dozens or even hundreds of opinions meeting in a crucible of ideas and goals. If managed effectively, it sparks growth and innovation.

When you encounter conflict, rather than allowing emotions to dictate your actions, use the DISC framework to analyze the situation. Ask yourself these questions: What behavioral style is each person exhibiting? What's the source of the disagreement? How does it relate to the different DISC styles at play? How can I express myself in a way that resonates with each style and facilitates resolution?

DISC in Conflict Management

Applying the DISC lens means that you no longer see conflict as a roadblock. Instead, you view it as an opportunity to deepen understanding, build empathy, and forge more robust, resilient relationships with team members. Let's explore some strategies and techniques that'll help you accomplish this.

1. **Understand your style.** Before attempting to resolve a conflict, we must first understand our own DISC style. This helps you recognize any biases you may have, and it also helps you approach conflict more objectively. For example, if you're a Dominance (D) style, you recognize that you tend to be quite assertive. Therefore, you need to work on being more receptive.

2. **Recognize the styles of others.** You then identify the styles of others involved in a conflict. This helps you understand their perspectives and communication styles, allowing you to tailor your approach to connect with them.

3. **Focus on behavior, not personality.** When discussing a conflict, focusing on specific behaviors rather than personalities is essential, as this keeps conversations objective. Avoid personal attacks or defensiveness. For example, if your conflict is with a Steadiness (S) individual, approach the situation calmly and with empathy. Say something like, "I noticed you missed the last three deadlines," rather than "You're always late."

4. **Use active listening.** Listening actively to others helps them feel heard, enabling you to understand their perspectives better. Paraphrase what they say and ask clarifying questions to show that you understand their position. Instead of jumping to conclusions, say, "Let me make sure I understood you correctly…"

5. **Seek common ground.** Look for areas of agreement or common ground between conflicting parties. This shifts the conversation from disagreement toward finding a solution. For instance, you both might agree that a project's success is the top priority.

6. **Brainstorm solutions.** Brainstorm potential solutions with the person you're in conflict with. Be open to their ideas and try to find solutions that meet both of your needs. Propose some middle ground by saying, "What if we try your method the next time, then compare the results?"

7. **Follow up.** After reaching a solution, follow up with the other individual to ensure that the conflict is resolved. A week or so later, you might ask, "How do you feel about the resolution we came up with? Is it working for you?"

With these strategies and techniques, individuals use their understanding of DISC to effectively resolve conflict and build stronger relationships within teams and organizations.

Unhealthy Conflict Styles

With conflict being inevitable in any team dynamic, how it's managed makes all the difference. Each style approaches conflict management with its own set of strengths and weaknesses. However, if left unchecked, these behaviors manifest in unhealthy ways.

For Dominance (D) individuals, their direct and assertive nature is often seen as aggressive and intimidating in conflict situations. They may bulldoze (or seem like they're bulldozing) others, prioritizing their goals at the expense of team harmony. For instance, a D-style individual might need to consider team feedback before pushing for their project proposal. D-style individuals often benefit from slowing down and listening to other people's perspectives before jumping into problem-solving mode.

The Influence (I) person's tendency to avoid conflict can lead to passive-aggressive behavior. It's also not uncommon for them to sugarcoat situations to keep everyone happy. For example, an I-style person might agree to a team decision in a meeting but express disagreement later behind the scenes. Therefore, I-style individuals benefit from developing the courage to speak up and address issues head-on (in the moment) instead of sacrificing authenticity to avoid conflict.

The Steadiness (S) person's desire for harmony and consensus can cause them to compromise their wants and needs during conflict. They may avoid expressing their true opinions, or acquiesce to the demands of others to maintain peace. An S-style team member might silently agree to a task they're uncomfortable with to avoid causing a stir. These individuals will benefit from learning to assert their needs and boundaries while valuing and respecting the needs of others.

The Conscientiousness (C) individual's focus on facts and details can lead to overanalyzing and nitpicking in conflict situations. They may become bogged down in small details, losing sight of the bigger picture and the overall emotional needs of the team. A C-style person might insist on correcting tiny inaccuracies in presentations while ignoring the overall message, thus causing unnecessary tension. C-style individuals benefit from understanding that sometimes the solution isn't just about the data but also the people involved.

Although each style features strengths and weaknesses for managing conflict, it's crucial to recognize when these behaviors become unhealthy. Individuals and teams build healthier and more effective conflict-management strategies by developing self-awareness and actively addressing these tendencies.

Onboarding Team Members

When onboarding team members, it's essential to understand and leverage the strengths of each DISC style. Below are some tips:

1. **Dominance (D) style.** People with a dominant style value confidence and results. Communicate the benefits and outcomes of projects and ideas to get them on your side. Show them how your ideas help them achieve their goals and solve problems. For example, if you propose a new sales strategy, focus on projected revenue growth and increased market share.

2. **Influence (I) style.** People who are good at influencing others value relationships and creativity. To get them on your side, show them how a project or idea will positively impact others and foster collaboration. Emphasize the potential for fun and excitement. If you propose a team-building activity, focus on how it will bring your team closer and create a positive, enjoyable experience.

3. **Steadiness (S) style.** People with a steady style value stability and harmony. Show them how your project or idea will maintain or improve the current situation. Emphasize the importance of a supportive team environment. For instance, if you're proposing a change in a process, focus on how it will create a streamlined and efficient workflow while maintaining the supportive culture they value.

4. **Conscientiousness (C) style.** People with a conscientiousness style value accuracy and precision. To gain their trust, show them your project or idea is well-thought-out and based on solid research and data. Emphasize attention to detail and the potential for continuous improvement. For example, if you're proposing a new product design, focus on the data and research that went into it, including how it'll improve overall functionality.

By understanding the preferences and values of each style, you tailor your communication style and approach to gain the trust of your team members.

Summary

The importance of navigating the different personalities in your team or organization illustrates the significance of effectively employing the DISC model in various scenarios—conflict resolution, recognizing unhealthy conflict behaviors, and gaining buy-in. Adapting your communication style and actions according to the DISC style of the person you're dealing with considerably enhances your conflict-management abilities. The four DISC styles—Dominance, Influence, Steadiness, and Conscientiousness—determine how an individual processes and responds to information. Understanding this helps you tailor your interactions to resonate with each style.

Equally important is the use of the DISC paradigm in conflict resolution. This helps individuals recognize the conflict styles of each DISC type and understand how they manifest in unhealthy ways. You address conflict objectively by identifying your own communication and conflict-management styles as well as those of others. You learn to focus on behavior over personality while seeking common ground and brainstorming mutual solutions.

Finally, using the DISC model to gain the trust of your team members is highly beneficial. By acknowledging and appealing to the values and preferences of each style, you ensure that everyone feels seen, heard, and appreciated. This approach fosters a harmonious and productive environment and paves the way for improved relationships and successful collaboration.

In the next chapter, we'll examine how to benefit from team feedback practices using the insights gained from the DISC framework. These best practices inspire growth, promote unity, and accelerate success.

Team Discussion Questions

1. Reflecting on your DISC style, can you identify any tendencies or biases you might bring into conflict situations? How do these influence your approach to resolving disagreements?

2. Have you observed any specific behaviors in your colleagues that align with their DISC styles? How have these behaviors influenced conflict dynamics within your team?

3. How can you use active listening and paraphrasing to ensure better understanding during conflict? Can you provide an example of when this could've changed the outcome of a past disagreement?

4. Considering each DISC style's unique strengths and weaknesses in conflict situations, can you identify an instance when an understanding of DISC could've helped you manage a conflict more effectively?

5. Discuss how your team can collectively leverage the DISC approach to find common ground in conflict scenarios. What steps can you take to ensure that this approach becomes a habit in your work environment?

6.
Feedback:
Giving and Receiving

With DISC as our guide, we transform feedback into
a shared compass, not a critique. It's a navigational
nudge, steering us closer to our collective success.
— Christopher Meade, PhD

Giving Better Feedback

The DISC focus creates a feedback feast. Understanding your team members' preferences and motivations (their styles) through DISC paves the way for more personalized, constructive feedback. As you dive into the tips below, keep an open mind and remain flexible to adapting your approach. Feedback isn't a one-size-fits-all process—it's a thoughtful practice that inspires growth, promotes unity, and encourages team success.

1. **Understand the person's DISC profile.** Before giving feedback, clearly understand a person's DISC profile. This helps you tailor your feedback to their communication and behavioral style. Avoid language or actions that may trigger a negative response.

2. **Use "I" statements.** Rather than making assumptions or pointing fingers, use "I" statements to express your observations and feelings. For example, "I noticed that I didn't receive updates on your progress when we were working on the project. I felt frustrated."

3. **Focus on specific behaviors.** Instead of generalizing or presuming about a person's character or motivations, focus on the specific behaviors that need to be addressed. This ensures that the conversation remains objective and focused.

4. **Offer actionable solutions.** Simply pointing out problems or issues can leave a person unsure of how to move forward. Offer specific, actionable solutions or suggestions for improvement.

5. **Follow up.** After giving feedback, check in with the person to see how they're doing, asking them if they have any questions or concerns. This keeps them feeling supported and motivated, and ready to make positive changes.

Effective feedback isn't about criticizing or blaming—it's about helping an individual learn and grow. With the DISC insights, you tailor your approach to the communication and behavioral style of others, and you create a more productive and positive feedback experience.

Tips for Giving and Receiving Feedback

Feedback can be tricky without proper (style) context. It's an essential part of personal and professional growth, but it can be challenging to provide feedback that's effective and well-received. Understanding the DISC styles helps you give and receive feedback in a way that resonates with each style. Here's how we navigate the four primary styles:

1. **Dominance (D) individuals value direct and straightforward communication.** Our feedback must be clear and concise with this person. Avoid beating around the bush or sugarcoating a message. For instance, if a D-style employee fails to meet deadlines, candidly approach them and

propose clear solutions for improvement. These individuals appreciate receiving feedback that's results-driven and focused on goals. When receiving feedback, D-styles prefer an assertive and direct approach. They want to quickly know what needs to be improved and how to get there.

2. **Influence (I) individuals value positive and encouraging feedback.** With this person, focus on what's working. Offer praise for accomplishments. For example, if an I-style team member successfully leads a project, commend their leadership and the positive energy they inspire. I-styles appreciate feedback that recognizes their strengths and contributions. When receiving feedback, they want to feel supported and validated. They appreciate positive feedback, as this emphasizes the value they bring to the team.

3. **Steadiness (S) individuals value supportive and personalized feedback.** Focus on building a relationship with this personality style. Show appreciation for these individuals. For instance, you could highlight an S-style employee's consistency in meeting project standards and their role in promoting team harmony. They appreciate nonconfrontational feedback that focuses on building trust and collaboration. When receiving feedback, S-styles prefer a supportive and caring approach. They want to feel valued and appreciated for their efforts.

4. **Conscientiousness (C) individuals value objective and data-driven feedback.** With this person, give specific examples and data to support your point. For instance, if a C-style worker has developed a thorough report, provide feedback on the beneficial specifics. Suggest areas they could improve on for depth and precision. C-styles appreciate feedback that's focused on improving processes and systems. When receiving feedback, they prefer a logical and

analytical approach. They want to understand the data and receive a clear improvement plan.

Providing tailored feedback improves its effectiveness. Because everyone has different preferences for giving and receiving feedback, understanding these differences leads to better communication and a more positive work environment.

Feedback to a Conscientiousness (C) Employee

Let's dive deeper on our tailored approach. Let's say you have a highly conscientious employee (C) who tends to be overly critical of themselves and others. Below are some tips on how to provide more effective feedback using DISC:

1. **Focus on their strengths.** We must first acknowledge their strengths and the value that they bring to the team. Start by praising them for their attention to detail, thoroughness, and accuracy.

2. **Address the behavior.** Next, address the specific behavior you want to change. In this case, you might say, "While I appreciate your attention to detail, I've noticed that you can be overly critical of yourself and others. This sometimes creates a negative team atmosphere. Let's see what we can do about that."

3. **Appeal to their values.** Because highly conscientious people tend to have solid values and beliefs, it helps to appeal to these when giving feedback. You might say, "I know how important it is for you to maintain high standards and deliver quality work. But, as we know, quality work also depends on a positive and supportive team environment. So let's ensure that we're focused on that while achieving goals."

4. **Provide specific suggestions.** Finally, provide specific recommendations for how they can improve their behavior. Some examples:

- Suggest that they focus on a situation's positive aspects or on finding solutions instead of dwelling on problems.

- Encourage them to balance their critical viewpoints with constructive feedback. You might say, "While it's great to identify problems, it could be beneficial for you and the team to provide potential solutions or suggestions for improvement when you spot an issue."

- Advise them to be more mindful of the way they communicate criticism. For instance, you can say, "I appreciate your eye for detail. However, framing criticisms in a more positive and supportive manner could be helpful. This would help team morale."

- Suggest that they put themselves in the shoes of the people they're criticizing. You might say, "I understand your commitment to high standards. However, it's important to consider your colleagues' perspectives and feelings when being critical. Remember, everyone is striving to do their best."

- Since they're also overly critical of themselves, advise them to practice self-compassion. For example, you could recommend, "While striving for excellence is important, it's also crucial to acknowledge that everyone, including yourself, makes mistakes. Try to learn from them and use them as stepping stones for growth rather than being overly critical of yourself."

- Recommend that they include their team members in problem solving. You might suggest, "When you notice an issue, instead of tackling it alone, consider bringing it to the team for discussion. This collaboration not only gives you more info to work with but it also fosters a more positive team environment."

When providing these suggestions, frame them in a way that maintains respect and appreciation for their conscientious nature.

Feedback to a Dominance (D) Employee

Now, let's say you have a highly dominant (D) employee who demonstrates strong leadership qualities but who also tends to make decisions without considering the feelings and input of others. Below are some tips on giving effective feedback using DISC:

1. **Focus on their strengths.** First, we acknowledge their strengths and the value that they bring to the team. Start by praising them for their decisiveness, goal-oriented nature, and ability to drive results.

2. **Address the behavior.** Next, address the specific behavior you want to change. In this case, you might say, "While I appreciate your leadership and decision-making skills, I've noticed that you can make decisions without considering the input or feelings of others. This can sometimes create tension within the team. Let's work on that."

3. **Appeal to their values.** Results and efficiency drive highly dominant individuals. Appeal to these values when giving feedback. You could say, "I know how important it is for you to achieve team goals quickly. However, it's also vital for us to maintain a harmonious and inclusive team environment to better achieve those goals."

4. **Provide specific suggestions.** Finally, provide specific recommendations for how they can improve their behavior. Some possibilities:

- Suggest that they try to include team members in the decision-making process more often. You could say, "Your leadership skills are appreciated, but it would benefit you and the team if you involve them in the decision-making process. It'll foster a more collaborative team environment."

- Encourage them to show empathy for team members. You might advise, "While it's essential to drive results, it's also important to consider the feelings and perspectives of your colleagues. Doing so increases team cohesion and morale."

- Practice active listening. For instance, you could say, "Your decisive nature is valuable, but listen actively to team member input before making decisions. This shows them that their contributions are valued."

- Suggest that they provide constructive feedback. You might say, "I understand your commitment to high standards. However, when providing feedback, try to balance the positive with suggestions for improvement. This approach helps create a more positive team environment."

- Recommend patience with the process. You could propose, "While striving for quick results is important, it's also crucial to acknowledge that some processes take time to ensure quality and inclusivity. Patience in these situations leads to more sustainable outcomes."

Feedback to a Steadiness (S) Employee

Let's say you have a highly steady (S) employee who tends to resist change and is slow to act. Below are some tips for giving them effective feedback using DISC:

1. **Focus on their strengths.** We first acknowledge their strengths and the value they bring to the team. Start by praising them for their dependability, consistency, and excellent listening skills.

2. **Address the behavior.** Next, address the specific behavior you want to change. In this case, you might say, "While I appreciate your consistency and dependability, I've noticed that you can be resistant to change and slow to act. This can sometimes hinder our team's progress and adaptability."

3. **Appeal to their values.** Because highly steady individuals value security and stability, it can be helpful to appeal to this in your feedback. You could say, "I understand and respect your need for stability and consistency. However, in our dynamic work environment, it's also crucial for us to adapt to change quickly."

4. **Provide specific suggestions.** Finally, provide detailed instructions for how they can improve their behavior. Some possible examples:

   - You might suggest that they work on their flexibility. For instance, "While your consistency is valuable, there are times when flexibility is necessary. Embracing change often leads to growth and new opportunities."

   - Encourage them to act more decisively. You could say, "While careful consideration is important, there are times when quick decisions are a must. Developing your ability to take action when necessary could greatly benefit the team."

- You might advise them to be more open to new ideas. For example, "Your commitment to maintaining stability is appreciated. However, new ideas and changes bring improvements that would benefit us all. Try to be more open to these possibilities."

- Suggest that they seek support when needed. You could say, "I understand that change can be challenging. Feel free to seek support or guidance when you're feeling uncertain. We're a team—we're here to help each other."

- Reassure them about change. Since they tend to resist it, assure them that it's sometimes necessary and beneficial. You might say, "Change can be unsettling, but it's crucial for growth and development. I promise to communicate changes clearly and timely, and we'll navigate them together as a team."

When providing these suggestions, frame them in a way that maintains respect and appreciation for their steady nature.

Feedback to an Influence (I) Employee

Let's say you have a highly influential (I) employee who tends to focus more on socializing and relationship building than completing tasks. Below are some tips on giving them more effective feedback using DISC:

1. **Focus on their strengths.** We first acknowledge their strengths and the value they bring to the team. Start by praising them for their excellent communication skills, ability to motivate others, and positive energy.

2. **Address the behavior.** Next, address the specific behavior you want to change. In this case, you might say, "While I appreciate your ability to build relationships and motivate others, I've noticed that you sometimes neglect your tasks due to excessive socializing. This sometimes affects team productivity."

3. **Appeal to their values.** Social recognition and group activities drive highly influential individuals, so appeal to these values when giving feedback. You could say, "I know how important it is for you to build strong team relationships and foster a positive work environment. However, it's also crucial for us to meet our deadlines and achieve our targets."

4. **Provide specific suggestions.** Finally, provide clear guidance on how they can improve their behavior. Some possible examples:

   - You might suggest that they work on balancing socializing and completing their tasks. For example, "While building relationships is great, meeting deadlines is also important. Perhaps scheduling specific time slots for socializing and working on tasks might help."

   - Encourage them to use their influencing skills to help the team achieve goals. You could say, "Your ability to motivate others is exceptional. Perhaps you could use this skill to boost morale and encourage others to meet deadlines."

   - Suggest they prioritize their tasks. You might say, "Your enthusiasm for building relationships is great, but remember to focus on your tasks. Prioritizing your tasks and scheduling your time effectively helps ensure that everything gets done on time."

- You could advise them to use their excellent communication skills to address work-related matters. For instance, "Your communication skills are outstanding. You should consider using them to facilitate more work-related discussions that enhance productivity."

- Recommend setting personal goals. Since they're highly motivated by achievement, advise them to set personal work goals. For example, "Setting daily or weekly goals for tasks might help you focus and manage your time more effectively."

Personalized Feedback Empowers Teams

The most effective feedback is personal—it fosters growth and team cohesion immeasurably. As a manager, you must understand the individual DISC styles of team members and adjust feedback accordingly. Being mindful of your members' traits, values, and behavioral tendencies allows you to provide feedback that resonates and motivates them to improve. You maintain a balance between positive reinforcement and constructive criticism, and keep the focus on behavior rather than personal attributes.

Also—and importantly—managers must be willing to receive as well as they give. Feedback is a two-way street, so encourage your team members to express their thoughts, feelings, and concerns. Not only will this help you understand their perspectives better but it will also create a culture of openness and mutual respect. Your ability to give and receive feedback significantly impacts your team's success and harmony. Remain patient, empathetic, and proactive in your feedback approach and you'll see the rewards reflected in the team's performance and morale.

Team Discussion Questions

1. How do you think understanding each other's DISC profiles helps you give and receive team feedback more effectively? Can you share a past example of how this knowledge could've made a difference?

2. We've learned that different DISC profiles prefer different types of feedback. How does this information change your perception about giving feedback? How could you adjust your feedback style according to the DISC profile of someone you're providing feedback to?

3. Looking at your DISC profile, do you agree with the suggested ways of receiving feedback? Why or why not? How can you tailor your approach to ensure that it resonates with your communication and behavioral style?

4. Reflecting on the tips for giving feedback, which tip do you find most challenging to implement, and why? How can you and your teammates support each other to improve feedback delivery?

5. Feedback is a two-way street, and fostering a culture of openness is essential. How comfortable do you feel expressing your thoughts, feelings, and concerns with your team? What steps can you take as a group to enhance comfort levels and promote open dialogue?

7.
Leading Effective Meetings

DISC doesn't just facilitate virtual meetings—it creates bridges between screens. In a world pixelated by distance, we tune into every person's wavelength, turning virtual spaces into a symphony of collaboration.

— Christopher Meade, PhD

Before the Meeting

Leaders know that meetings can be tricky and complex affairs. These interactions—whether large-scale, all-hands-on-deck staff meetings, intimate one-on-one discussions, or dynamic virtual conferences—are crucial to boosting collaboration, cultivating relationships, and achieving exceptional business outcomes. But it's no secret that effectively conducting them can be challenging. This collaborative and fertile ground can, however, be plowed much more efficiently and sympathetically while using the DISC "style" model.

So let's adapt our communication strategies to engage and motivate "styled" team members in this group setting. We're going to transform meetings from mundane tasks into engaging, productive, and inclusive seminars that inspire members more personally. From here on out, your meetings will consist of tailored interactions that bring out the best in everyone.

Engaging Virtual Meetings

Virtual meetings are now an essential part of many professionals' lives, but they can be pretty challenging to navigate—especially when it comes to understanding others and communicating effectively. Using DISC in virtual meetings, however, allows you to effectively understand and connect with your members on a personal level, leading to more productive and successful meetings. Let's dive in.

1. **Start with an assessment.** Before your meeting, have team members take a DISC assessment, which will provide valuable information about each person's communication style and behavioral tendencies. With this information, you can better understand each other and tailor communication accordingly.

2. **Use DISC language.** During the meeting, use the language of DISC to describe your communication style and identify the others' styles. For example, someone high in Dominance may be characterized as direct, assertive, and results-oriented, while someone high in Steadiness may be identified as supportive, patient, and a good listener.

3. **Tailor your communication style.** Based on the assessment results, tailor your communication style to each person's preferences. For example, someone high in Influence appreciates a more personal touch, whereas someone high in Conscientiousness appreciates more detail-oriented, data-driven communication.

4. **Manage conflict.** The DISC lens helps manage conflict in virtual meetings. When you understand the communication style of each individual, you can better anticipate where conflict may arise and take steps to prevent it. You can also tailor conflict-resolution strategies to the style of each member.

5. **Use nonverbal participation.** Use the chat function to engage C-style members who prefer to communicate through writing rather than speaking. Encourage them to share their ideas and thoughts in the chat box, and then acknowledge and address their comments during meetings.

6. **Plan.** Before meetings, send out an agenda, including any necessary documents or materials, to D and C-style team members, as they like to be prepared and focused. This satiates their data appetite and allows them to attend meetings ready to act.

7. **Get creative.** Use visual aids, such as graphs, charts, and images, to engage I-style members, as they're creative and enjoy visual stimulation. This keeps them engaged and interested in discussions.

8. **Employ wait times.** Give S-style members ample time to express their opinions and feelings during meetings. They prefer to build relationships and maintain harmony, so creating a safe and supportive environment for them to speak up is essential.

9. **Use DISC to set communication expectations.** Before virtual meetings, each team member should share their communication style and preferences using DISC, helping everyone understand how to communicate effectively with one another in real time. For instance, a team member with a Dominance style (D) would prefer direct and concise communication. An individual with an Influence (I) profile favors an engaging and interactive approach. Those high in Steadiness (S) prefer a more supportive and empathetic tone. And a person with a Conscientiousness style (C) appreciates detailed and analytical discussions. Understanding these different preferences allows for more effective and inclusive communication during meetings.

10. **Take advantage of breakout rooms and small group discussions.** This ensures that all team members have a chance to contribute and participate regardless of DISC style.

By using the DISC framework in virtual meetings, you can better understand and connect with your colleagues, leading to productive and successful meetings. By tailoring your communication style and conflict-resolution strategies to the preferences of each individual, you create a more inclusive and effective virtual-meeting environment.

Enhanced One-On-One Meetings

Individualized meetings allow managers to build rapport and cultivate deeper relationships with employees. Using the DISC model to understand your employees' communication styles helps you tailor your approach and make the most of these conversations. Consider the following when engaging in one-on-one meetings with those steeped in each of the four DISC styles:

1. **D-style: direct and dominant.** When meeting with a D-style employee, you cut to the chase and focus on the bottom line. They want to see progress, results, and efficiency. Keep the conversation on track and avoid getting bogged down with small talk and petty details. They appreciate a direct, no-nonsense approach. Be prepared with concrete examples of how their work contributes to the organization's goals. D-style team members may feel frustrated with perceived inefficiency, such as meetings that lack a clear agenda or veer off-topic. Don't feed that frustration with meetings that focus more on small talk than task-oriented discussions.

2. **I-style: interactive and influential.** I-style employees thrive on social interaction and personal connections. Begin conversations by asking how they're doing, and be prepared to

engage in friendly banter. Give them plenty of opportunity to share their thoughts and ideas. They value recognition and appreciation, so give them positive feedback. I-style individuals may feel frustrated during meetings if they lack opportunities to express their thoughts. They might find formal meetings with little room for brainstorming or interactive discussion to be draining and disheartening.

3. **S-style: steady and supportive.** S-style colleagues value stability and a sense of belonging. Start by acknowledging their contributions to the team and creating a comfortable, low-pressure environment. Although they prefer to work steadily, don't overwhelm them with too many topics or changes at once. They value sincere feedback, so give them positive reinforcement and constructive criticism. S-style people might feel stressed and frustrated in meetings that involve abrupt changes, confrontation, or an overly aggressive pace. They may feel drained if they're forced to rush through their thought process.

4. **C-style: cautious and conscientious.** C-style associates value accuracy and attention to detail. They tend to be more reserved and analytical, so avoid making rash decisions or being too informal. Provide plenty of data and facts to support your points, as they value clear guidelines and expectations. Be specific about what you need from them, and be patient and willing to listen to their ideas and concerns. C-style individuals may feel frustrated in meetings where decisions are made hastily without thorough analysis or if logical reasoning or data is lacking. They find it draining when you expect them to make quick decisions without giving them time to analyze all the available information.

We can see how the DISC profile enhances the effectiveness of one-on-one meetings. By comprehending each style's communication preferences, you tailor your approach to facilitate open, honest, and productive conversation. Not only does this understanding allow you to steer clear of situations that cause frustration but it also enables you to meet each team member where they're most comfortable. The respect and empathy reflected through this approach can nurture trust and rapport.

When every team member feels valued and understood, you open the door to greater collaboration, increased productivity, and deeper relationships. Employing the DISC model creates an environment of mutual respect and understanding, empowering each team member to communicate in a way that resonates with them. Harnessing the power of DISC to guide one-on-one meetings leads to improved results and a harmonious work environment. Better understanding leads to better communication, which, in turn, drives better outcomes.

All-Hands Meetings and Staff Meetings

Adapting your approach to cater to each DISC style in all-hands meetings and staff meetings significantly enhances engagement and overall effectiveness. Here's how you address each DISC style more thoroughly:

1. **Dominance.** D-style team members thrive in goal-oriented environments, focusing on accomplishing tasks and achieving results. Keep meetings concise and centered around crucial objectives. Let them have a say in driving action plans forward. When assigning roles, tap into their natural inclination to lead and solve problems. Acknowledge their achievements and progress in front of team members, which reinforces their motivation. For instance, you might say, "Taylor, your relentless effort on the latest project helped us close the deal ahead of schedule. Great job leading that."

2. **Influence.** I-style team members are social, enthusiastic, people-focused individuals who love being in the center of the action. Kick off meetings energetically and make room for lighthearted interaction. Make space for them to share their experiences and ideas, and engage their creative minds by encouraging brainstorming sessions. Promote tasks that allow them to present and interact with others. Give compliments such as, "Anna, your engaging presentation brought our marketing plan to life. Thanks for the creative approach."

3. **Steadiness.** S-style colleagues value harmony and teamwork, so create a supportive and inclusive atmosphere. Provide room for personal updates, and don't rush or interrupt them when they speak. Clearly express their value to the team and assign roles that maintain harmony, support others, and build consensus. Offer a compliment like, "Nicole, your calm and steady approach in handling customer service issues has improved client satisfaction. Your hard work doesn't go unnoticed."

4. **Conscientiousness.** C-style team members appreciate structure, precision, and thoughtful and logical decision making. Begin with a clear agenda and a detailed overview of the topics you plan to discuss. Encourage them to question, analyze, and offer expert input, as they excel in tasks requiring meticulous planning, data analysis, or adherence to standards. Acknowledging their dedication could be as simple as saying, "Emily, your detailed analysis helped us make a sound decision on that challenging project."

Understanding and accommodating each DISC style ensures that every team member feels acknowledged and valued, and it creates an environment of trust and respect, leading to more successful and productive staff meetings. Allowing everyone to function in their natural communication style reinforces a more cohesive and efficient team dynamic, strengthening your organization's overall performance.

Summary

Drawing from the insights into each DISC style, we see that effective communication works in all group scenarios: all-hands meetings, staff meetings, one-on-one meetings, and virtual gatherings. Each is significantly enhanced by understanding and adapting to the DISC profiles of your team.

Each team member—be they the Dominance, Influence, Steadiness, or Conscientiousness style—has strengths and communication preferences that you harness to make meetings more successful. Your role as a manager is to create an environment that caters to these diverse styles and tastes, promoting better engagement, more productive discussions, and a more cohesive team. By recognizing and acknowledging these traits, you elevate the effectiveness of your meetings and build a culture of respect and understanding beyond the boardroom.

With every team member being a blend of different DISC styles, successful communication lies in recognizing and leveraging these complexities. You'll find yourself more capable of effectively navigating meetings through practice, patience, and consistently applying these insights.

In the next chapter, we'll focus on another crucial application of this framework—DISC-based interviewing. It's a technique that'll revolutionize your approach to hiring and selecting suitable candidates for your team.

Team Discussion Questions

1. How do you identify with each DISC style—Dominance, Influence, Steadiness, and Conscientiousness—in the context of meetings? How might understanding your style influence how you act across various meeting types?

2. Given your understanding of your DISC style, what steps can you take to adapt your communication style to better engage with colleagues with different DISC profiles? Can you provide examples from your experience?

3. How did you handle conflict in past virtual meetings? Reflecting on your experience, how might applying DISC conflict-resolution strategies affect the outcome of those situations?

4. Considering the unique characteristics of each DISC style, how can you tailor all-hands meetings and staff meetings to ensure that everyone feels acknowledged and valued? Can you think of any specific changes that might improve team meetings?

5. Reflecting on one-on-one meetings, how would understanding the DISC style of another team member change your approach or the outcome of a past meeting? How will you prepare for future one-on-one sessions?

8.
Interview Questions: Using DISC for Discovery

Concerning interviews, DISC is like having a map of the unseen—it guides us through motivation, stress, and individual work preferences, painting a vivid picture of a candidate's journey.

— Christopher Meade, PhD

Rooting Out Their "Style"

While interviewing job candidates, you want to assess more than just their professional qualifications—you want to know if their personality and style match the demands of the role and culture of your organization. The DISC behavioral assessment focuses on the four distinct personality traits: Dominance (D), Influence (I), Steadiness (S), and Conscientiousness (C).

By posing questions designed to unveil a candidate's DISC style, you gain a clear picture of how they might behave, what motivates them, and how they may respond to stress. The following 20 questions were designed to prompt responses that reveal a candidate's DISC profile.

1. **Describe when you had to work with a team to complete a project. How did you approach this situation, and what was the outcome?**

   DISC Insight: This question helps you learn whether a candidate is I style (Influence) or S style (Steadiness), who may thrive in team environments; D style (Dominance), who might prefer individual tasks; or C style (Conscientious), who may indicate their meticulous contribution to the team.

2. **How do you handle conflict with others in the workplace? Can you give an example?**

   DISC Insight: This question can uncover whether a candidate leans toward the typically assertive D style, accommodating S style, diplomatic I style, or methodical C style during conflict.

3. **What motivates you to work hard and achieve your goals?**

   DISC Insight: Their answer may reveal their drive. D style is generally driven by achievement and control, I style by social recognition, S style by stability and cooperation, and C style by correctness and quality.

4. **Describe your communication style. How do you tailor communication to different individuals or groups?**

   DISC Insight: This could reveal a flexible communicator who can adapt to different styles. D styles might be direct, I styles engaging and enthusiastic, S styles diplomatic and warm, and C styles precise and fact-oriented.

5. **How do you prioritize tasks and manage time effectively?**

   DISC Insight: This may indicate if a candidate is a typically task-oriented D style, a C style who is generally well-organized, or a usually people-oriented I or S style who may need to work on time management.

6. **Describe a situation where you had to be flexible and adapt to change.**

   DISC Insight: Adaptability is generally a strong suit of I and D styles, while S and C styles usually prefer stability and predictability.

7. **How do you handle criticism and negative feedback?**

   DISC Insight: C and D styles may appreciate feedback focused on tasks, while I and S styles tend to prefer feedback focused on relationships and tone.

8. **Describe your problem-solving approach. How do you gather information and evaluate options?**

   DISC Insight: D styles might be decisive and quick, I styles might seek the opinions of others, S styles might be careful and steady, and C styles might be analytical and thorough in problem solving.

9. **How do you build and maintain relationships with co-workers and clients?**

   DISC Insight: I styles will generally be naturally strong in this area, while D styles may be more task-focused. S styles tend to foster harmonious relationships, and C styles usually build relationships based on competence and quality.

10. **Can you describe a situation where you had to take a risk to achieve a goal? What was the outcome?**

    DISC Insight: D and I styles might be more comfortable taking risks, while S and C styles generally prefer caution and thoroughness.

11. How do you handle stress in the workplace?

DISC Insight: D styles might thrive under pressure, I styles might seek social support, S styles might prefer a stable environment, and C styles might focus on planning and analyzing.

12. Describe a time when you had to take on a leadership role. How did you approach the situation, and what was the outcome?

DISC Insight: D styles might demonstrate assertive leadership, I styles might show collaborative leadership, S styles might display supportive leadership, and C styles might exhibit analytical leadership.

13. How do you handle tasks or projects outside your comfort zone or expertise?

DISC Insight: D styles might show a willingness to tackle new challenges, I styles might seek help from others, S styles might prefer working within their comfort zone, and C styles might rely on thorough learning and preparation.

14. Describe your decision-making process. How do you weigh the pros and cons of different options?

DISC Insight: D styles might make decisions quickly, I styles might consider the impact on people, S styles might be cautious and seek consensus, and C styles might rely on data and analysis.

15. How do you handle setbacks or failures in the workplace?

DISC Insight: D styles might be resilient and see failure as an opportunity, I styles might maintain a positive attitude, S styles might prefer steady progress to avoid setbacks, and C styles might analyze what went wrong to prevent future mistakes.

16. Describe your approach to learning and self-improvement.

DISC Insight: D styles might seek knowledge to improve their results, I styles might enjoy learning in social settings, S styles might prefer a structured learning environment, and C styles might want deep dives into complex topics.

17. How do you handle changes or disruptions in your routine or work environment?

DISC Insight: D and I styles might adapt to change easily, whereas S and C styles often prefer routine and may require more time to adjust to change.

18. Describe a time when you had to use creative thinking or problem-solving to overcome a challenge.

DISC Insight: I and D styles might show more comfort with creative, out-of-the-box thinking, while S and C styles might prefer more traditional, tried-and-true solutions.

19. How do you handle competition in the workplace?

DISC Insight: D styles might thrive in it, I styles might see competition as a chance for collaboration, S styles might prefer cooperation over competition, and C styles might focus on meeting high standards rather than direct competition.

20. Describe your leadership style, including how you motivate and inspire others.

DISC Insight: D styles might lead through authority and results, I styles through enthusiasm and relationships, S styles through steadiness and support, and C styles through expertise and quality.

Summary

DISC-based interview questions allow you to dive beneath the qualifications listed on a resume to better understand a candidate's work style and personality. They give you crucial insight into how the candidate handles conflict, their communication style, how they react under stress, their problem-solving approach, and their ability to work within a team setting. Understanding these traits helps you predict a candidate's fit within your company's culture and role.

The DISC assessment provides nuanced knowledge, but it isn't intended to be comprehensive. Use it as just one of the many tools in your toolbox to help gain a holistic picture of a candidate's potential. The insight you gain from these questions plays a significant role in making informed hiring decisions, and it contributes to successful long-term employee retention and team integration.

Now that we've explored the benefits of DISC interviewing, let's dive into the next chapter to discover the art form that helps you understand, connect, and communicate more effectively with people—the art of people reading.

Team Discussion Questions

1. Have you been using DISC assessments in your past interviewing process? Can you identify any patterns in the candidates you tend to select? Do they correlate with specific DISC styles?

2. How does your team's current DISC composition affect your work environment? Are there any DISC styles that dominate? How does this influence team dynamics and performance?

3. How could you tailor your interview questions to discern a candidate's DISC profile better? Can you think of additional questions that might unveil specific DISC traits more effectively?

4. When considering a candidate's DISC style, how much weight should it carry in the overall decision-making (hiring) process? How might you balance these insights with other factors, such as professional qualifications and experience?

5. How does understanding a candidate's DISC style assist in onboarding and integrating them into the team? What strategies can you implement to align team members with different DISC profiles to enhance collaboration and productivity?

9.
People Reading:
Let's Do Some Exercises

Through the lens of DISC, we learn the language of human behavior, transforming strangers into familiar faces and every interaction into an opportunity for connection.

— Christopher Meade, PhD

Our DISC model, in a few of the previous chapters, might just as easily be called "the boomerang model." You toss out lots of questions to workers and job candidates, and their answers come flying back at you, providing profound insight into their style, their personality, and where they may fit in the wonderful workplace panoply. Asking the questions greatly enhances our understanding and interaction with others, and it lets us know where they may stand in the four DISC types: Dominance, Influence, Steadiness, and Conscientiousness. In this chapter, however, we keep our questions to ourselves, inside our own mind, as we mentally evaluate the sea of extraordinary styles around us.

When engaging in dynamic environments, such as cross-functional teams or meeting with various external stakeholders, we often lack the time and means to learn people's DISC assessment results. Also, we constantly interact with individuals from diverse backgrounds and cultures who may not be familiar with the DISC model. In these settings, an educated guess regarding someone's DISC type is indispensable. In other words, we must people read.

That doesn't mean we're unfairly judging or making definitive assumptions about someone's personality—on the contrary. People reading is about building bridges of understanding, generating deeper connections, and enhancing our ability to communicate and collaborate more effectively. This is particularly crucial in today's globalized world, where success often hinges on our ability to understand and connect with a wide range of individuals, each with unique behaviors, preferences, and communication styles.

Observation, Differentiation, Confirmation

We'll follow a structured "reading" approach based on observation, differentiation, and confirmation, recognizing behavioral patterns aligned with DISC types. This allows us to form a nuanced understanding of the individuals we interact with and helps us communicate with them.

As much as we provide structure to this "reading," we must remember that this exercise serves as an observational approach rather than a precise measurement akin to an actual DISC assessment. It helps us recognize tendencies, but it doesn't capture a person's full complexity and diversity. We must also keep in mind that it's normal for people to exhibit traits from more than one DISC type, highlighting the multidimensional (complex) nature of human behavior.

By honing our people-reading skills, we equip ourselves with a valuable compass to navigate the interpersonal landscape of our personal and professional lives more effectively. As we refine our understanding of those around us, we can tailor our communication style, foster positive relationships, and enhance our collective success.

Below, an in-depth DISC guide to people reading:

1. Observation

Observe a person's behavior in different situations. See how they communicate, make decisions, react under pressure, and interact with others. Some questions to ask yourself:

1. **Dominance (D) Style:**
   - Do they take initiative in discussions or tasks, demonstrating a "take charge" attitude?
   - Do they tend to speak more than they listen during conversation?
   - How do they react when faced with obstacles or challenges? Do they tend to confront them directly?
   - Do they prioritize results and goals over processes and relationships?
   - Are they comfortable with risk taking and pushing boundaries to achieve their objectives?

2. **Influence (I) Style:**
   - Do they use stories, humor, and expressive gestures when communicating?
   - Do they have a broad social circle and engage easily in small talk?
   - How do they react when the spotlight is on them? Do they enjoy being the center of attention?
   - Do they show an affinity for team activities and group projects?
   - Are they usually optimistic and enthusiastic? Do they influence others with their energy?

3. **Steadiness (S) Style:**
   - Do they show patience and empathy for the viewpoints of others during interactions?

- How do they handle abrupt changes or unexpected problems? Do they remain composed and maintain harmony?

- Are they attentive listeners, often allowing others to speak before they do?

- Are they more supportive and less competitive in team interactions?

- How do they approach deadlines and fast-paced situations? Do they prefer a more relaxed and planned environment?

4. **Conscientiousness (C) Style:**

- Do they tend to analyze situations carefully before making decisions?

- Do they value precision, accuracy, and thoroughness in their work and communication?

- How do they approach rules and structure? Do they adhere strictly or prefer flexibility?

- Are they generally more reserved and introspective, often observing before participating in discussions?

- How do they handle criticism and feedback? Do they see it as an opportunity to improve and perfect their work?

"The code is more what you'd call *guidelines* than actual rules," says the famous pirate Barbossa from *Pirates of the Caribbean*—and so it goes with our DISC approach to "reading" a person's style. As we use the insightful DISC, we must keep this in mind and remember that people are complex, often displaying characteristics from multiple DISC styles. We're not labeling or stereotyping—we're understanding and respecting individual differences in behavior while using our guidelines.

2. Differentiation

Now that you've observed their behavior, you should understand pretty well where they *don't* fit—which DISC type they are *not*. Differentiation. Perhaps they're assertive and direct (Dominance) but not particularly detail-oriented or reserved (Conscientiousness). If they're social and persuasive, they could be high in Influence, but if they're not exceptionally patient or cooperative, Steadiness might not be a match.

During the differentiating phase, you want to *exclude* the DISC styles least likely to align with the individual's behavior. You'll likely have a few initial impressions of their primary DISC type, but there might be more than one type that seems plausible.

Differentiating is a refining process in which you further investigate those initial impressions to identify potential inconsistencies. Look for contradictions between the person's behavior and the typical characteristics of each DISC style. (All of the above helps prevent presumption.)

Below are some key aspects and questions to consider during differentiation:

1. **Review your observations and impressions.** Reflect on the behavior you noticed and your initial thoughts about it. Ask yourself: Are there any glaring inconsistencies between these and the typical traits of each DISC style?

2. **Determine possible mismatches.** Try to identify behaviors that might contradict a particular DISC style. For example, if someone is highly people-oriented and expressive, they might not be a match for the Conscientiousness type, which is typically more reserved and task-oriented.

3. **Analyze their communication style.** How does the person communicate? Are they more direct or indirect? Do

they prioritize logic or emotions in conversation? This helps rule out specific DISC styles. For instance, a direct and logic-focused communicator might not align with the Influence style, which typically favors a more emotional and persuasive manner.

4. **Consider their approach to challenges.** How does the person handle obstacles and pressure? Someone who avoids confrontation and prefers harmony is less likely to be a Dominance type, generally known for their direct and assertive approach to challenges.

5. **Examine their comfort level with rules and structure.** If a person frequently pushes boundaries and challenges the status quo, they might not align with the Steadiness or Conscientiousness styles, which typically value consistency, rules, and structure.

6. **Reflect on their decision-making process.** Do they make quick, decisive decisions, or do they prefer to take their time, considering every angle before choosing a path? This helps rule out certain styles. For example, if they're more methodical and cautious when making decisions, they might not be a Dominance type, typically characterized by quick and assertive decision making.

By reflecting on these questions and considering an individual's behavior in different contexts, you can more accurately eliminate the DISC types that don't align with their style. This process of elimination (differentiation) leaves you with the DISC styles that are most likely to fit, which you can then confirm (or adjust) in the next phase of evaluation.

3. Confirmation

Confirmation is your final stage of the people-reading exercise, validating the one or two DISC types you winnowed during the elimination process. Here you'll gather additional evidence that potentially supports your initial assessment.

Below are some specific approaches to bolster the confirmation process:

1. **Continued observation.** Monitor the person's behavior in various contexts over a more extended period. Their myriad reactions in different situations provide crucial insight. For instance, how do they handle conflict? How do they perform in group settings? How do they respond to changes or unexpected situations? These observations provide more data points to confirm their specific DISC type (or types).

2. **Reflection.** Reflect on your overall impressions of the person. Which behaviors stood out the most? Which characteristics align most clearly with a specific DISC type?

3. **Ask hypothetical questions.** To enhance the people reading, you may pose hypothetical situations that provoke reactions relevant to different DISC types. For example, you could ask them how they'd handle an urgent project with a tight deadline to see if they take a dominant, decisive approach (D) or a steady, organized one (S). You could also ask how they'd manage a situation where a colleague disagrees with them to see if their approach is more influential, fostering a discussion and consensus (I), or conscientious, focusing on data and correctness (C).

4. **Directly seek feedback.** If your relationship allows, ask them how they see themselves—their self-perceived behaviors and preferences. Their self-perception might provide valuable insights, helping you confirm their DISC type.

5. **Peer feedback.** Seek feedback from others who interact with the person regularly. Multiple perspectives help avoid bias and provide a more well-rounded understanding of the person's behavior.

6. **Cross-check with other models.** If you're familiar with other personality models (such as the Big Five, Myers-Briggs, Enneagram, StrengthsFinder, etc.), you could cross-check their behavior with these frameworks for further confirmation.

7. **Reflect on their motivations.** Different motivators drive each DISC type, so understanding what drives a person can be revealing. For instance, people high in Dominance are often motivated by control over their environment and outcomes, whereas those high in Steadiness are typically driven by peace and stability.

Summary

Mastering the DISC people-reading exercise hones your assessment skills, providing insight that leads to deeper connections and fruitful collaboration—precipitating even greater empathy and respect for your colleagues. You understand people's nuances and appreciate their unique way of thinking, behaving, and interacting. Now, you can adapt your communication style and behavior to acknowledge and respect their nuances and differences.

No, you haven't boxed individuals into static categories. You've fostered understanding, tolerance, and mutual respect among diverse individuals and teams. DISC people reading isn't about arriving at an irrevocable conclusion—it's about learning, adapting, and growing in interpersonal relationships.

Applying the DISC model enhances your capacity to navigate the complexities of human behavior, fostering an environment of understanding, respect, and effective communication. Each time you practice and refine this skill, you take a step toward becoming a better colleague, leader, and communicator, contributing positively to the communities and organizations you're a part of. Carefully and properly reading the people around us makes them *and* us more amenable.

It's time to journey onto the final chapter, where we'll consolidate insights, reflect on their significance, and explore how you use them to craft a more empathetic, understanding, and effective workplace environment.

Team Discussion Questions

1. How relevant is the DISC model to your team dynamics? What are some instances when understanding each other's DISC types could've improved communication or collaboration?

2. How can you effectively incorporate the principles of people reading to enhance understanding and respect for individual differences in behavior? Can you think of an instance when people reading might've been beneficial in the past?

3. People reading involves three key stages: observation, differentiation, and confirmation. Which of these should you focus on most as a team? Can you provide an example that illustrates your point?

4. When using people reading as a tool, we must remember that individuals often exhibit traits from more than one DISC type. How do you think this complexity impacts team interactions and decision-making processes? Discuss a situation where this multidimensional nature of human behavior was evident.

5. How can the practice of people reading support you in adapting your communication style to better engage with diverse team members and stakeholders? Describe a situation where adapting communication styles according to the DISC model could've led to a better outcome.

10.
The DISC Dynamo:
Empowering Leadership
& Team Harmony

DISC isn't merely a lens to view behavior with. It's a compass guiding us through the wilderness of team dynamics and leadership, turning obstacles into opportunities for growth and understanding.
— Christopher Meade, PhD

Just as a disc is round, so have we circumnavigated 'round the ubiquitous personalities and relationships of work life with DISC. In doing so, we've illuminated the path toward empowered leadership, trust building, healthy communication, conflict management, giving and receiving feedback, leading effective meetings, accurately reading people, and facilitating engaging team activities. As we reach the end of our journey, let's take a moment to reflect on the knowledge we've gained.

Empowered leadership understands and values the diversity of teams, so the DISC model is perfect for such leaders. We can identify the unique behavioral styles of team members, enabling them to excel in their strengths and contribute to a shared vision.

Trust building is deeply intertwined with understanding and appreciating others. The DISC model helps us recognize the motivations and fears of team members, promoting an environment of trust where everyone feels seen, understood, and appreciated.

Our section on healthy communication illustrated the role of DISC in crafting harmonious team dialogue. Understanding our communication style and those of team members allows us to build bridges and nurture open and respectful discussion.

In conflict management, we learned how the DISC model helps us predict potential friction points—and how to navigate them. By understanding behavioral styles, we manage conflict constructively and cultivate growth and cooperation within our teams.

On giving and receiving feedback, the DISC model tailors our approach to the unique behavioral styles of team members. Recognizing these distinct styles allows us to provide feedback that's not only well-received but that also fosters growth and improvement. It also helps us understand how to receive feedback from others, turning constructive criticism into valuable learning opportunities.

The DISC model enables us to more accurately read people and decipher our teammates' behavioral cues more effectively. Now we can anticipate their needs, reactions, and preferences, enabling us to lead and communicate more effectively. By accurately reading people, we promote a work environment that's responsive, empathetic, and inclusive.

Conducting meetings with DISC, we recognize how different "styles" contribute to the discussion and atmosphere. This allows us to facilitate productive, engaging discussions where we're respectful of everyone's time and input.

In all activities, the DISC model provides a unique framework to engage teams, build strong relationships, and improve collaboration. By considering the DISC styles of team members, we tailor activities to their strengths, needs, and motivations.

Final Thoughts

Taken as a whole, the DISC model transcends professional spaces. It's an invaluable resource for personal growth that helps us understand our behavioral preferences and improve our relationships outside the workplace. As we learn to recognize and appreciate the distinct styles in our personal lives, we expand our capacity for empathy, deepen our relationships, and enrich our life experiences.

Of course, the DISC framework isn't static. It offers flexibility and allows our styles to shift depending on environment and circumstances. As we progress through our leadership journey, we must continually reflect on our evolving style and the evolving styles of others—and so the DISC model becomes an integral part of our growth and development as leaders.

And what's a journey without companions? Let's remember that effective leadership isn't a solitary endeavor. It's a collaborative adventure that involves learning from and with your team. The beauty of the DISC framework lies in its ability to highlight the unique contributions of each team member, illustrating the importance of every individual in team success. As we continue to foster an environment that values diversity and cultivates trust, we build high-performing teams and become better leaders.

As we close this chapter, allow what you've learned to permeate your actions, guide your decisions, and inspire you to become a compassionate, understanding, and effective leader. Though the journey may be challenging, with the DISC model as your compass, you can navigate the complexities of leadership and team dynamics.

11.
Boosting Team Dynamics: 20 Team Activities Using DISC

Through the lens of DISC, team activities become a vibrant tapestry of collaboration—every thread unique, every pattern essential—fostering a team dynamic that's stronger, richer, and more colorful than ever before.

— Christopher Meade, PhD

Explore the diverse range of human behaviors with these small-group activities focusing on DISC communication. Each exercise provides a vibrant mosaic of personality styles, helping you (the facilitator) better understand yourself and others, leading to more effective teamwork.

1. Navigating the Four Corners

Purpose: This team activity is a visual and interactive way to demonstrate team members' various DISC styles and personality traits. The Four Corners activity is a dynamic tool that promotes self-discovery and enhances team synergy, nurturing a deeper appreciation for colleagues' distinctive strengths and perspectives.

Instructions:

1. As the facilitator, begin by transforming the room's four corners into physical representations of the DISC styles—Dominance, Influence, Steadiness, and Conscientiousness. Place a sign in each corner that indicates each style.

2. Unveil the intricate tapestry of each DISC style, explaining its respective behaviors, strengths, and weaknesses. You might prompt your team with, "Can you think of a public figure who exemplifies each of these styles? How do they interact with others?"

3. Invite participants to do some introspection. Ask them to gravitate toward the corner of the room that best mirrors their personality style. If some participants resonate with multiple styles, the center of the room is the perfect spot.

4. With everyone comfortably nestled in their corners, it's time to orchestrate a lively discussion about each style. Facilitate prompts like, "Share a time when your style's strengths shone through at work" or "How does your style's potential weakness challenge you?" This collective exploration of experiences and insights is critical to demystifying the complexities of the various communication styles, work preferences, and unique team strengths.

5. After the initial discussion, channel the conversation into a debrief session. Together, analyze the advantages of having a team as diverse as a painter's palette. Strategize about how to optimize communication and collaboration across different styles. You could ask, "What can we learn from each other's styles? How can we better adapt our communication to work together more seamlessly?"

Big Idea: The Four Corners activity illuminates the richness of personality styles within teams. It catalyzes self-awareness and mutual understanding, and it fosters a culture of appreciation for the unique strengths of others.

Outcome: Upon completing this activity, you'll notice a palpable shift in your team's dynamics. Understanding is the first step to acceptance, and that's exactly what this activity is designed to do. It lays the groundwork for improved communication, collaboration, and understanding, enabling teams to work harmoniously.

Team Q&A: Below are five potential questions you can expect to encounter while leading this exercise, along with helpful responses to each:

Question 1: What if I don't wholly identify with any of the four corners?

Answer 1: That's completely normal. The DISC model represents a spectrum of behaviors, and you can exhibit traits from multiple styles. You may stand in the center of the room if you resonate with numerous styles. This is the beauty of this exercise; it shows that everyone's personality is unique and nuanced, not strictly confined to a single category.

Question 2: How does understanding different DISC styles benefit our team?

Answer 2: Understanding different DISC styles significantly improves team dynamics. It fosters a deeper understanding and appreciation of your colleagues' unique strengths and perspectives, enhancing communication and collaboration, as well as reducing misunderstanding and conflict. It highlights everyone's strengths and helps us understand how to communicate and work together effectively.

Question 3: Do our DISC styles change over time?

Answer 3: While your core DISC personality traits tend to remain stable, your behavior can change based on your environment, experience, and personal growth. You may also express different aspects of your personality in various contexts—for example, at work or home.

Question 4: How can we use our understanding of DISC to communicate more effectively with the team?

Answer 4: Knowing the DISC styles of your team members helps you tailor your communication to be more effective. For example, D-style people prefer direct, concise contact, while I styles enjoy a personal conversational approach. S styles value a supportive and collaborative delivery, and C styles appreciate detailed, accurate, and objective information. You can communicate more effectively with each team member by understanding and respecting these preferences.

Question 5: I'm concerned about the potential for bias if we label each other with DISC styles. How can we prevent this?

Answer 5: That's a valid concern. It's crucial to remember that DISC isn't about boxing people into rigid categories but understanding and appreciating differences. Each style has its strengths and potential areas for growth. Nobody is "better" or "worse" based on their DISC style. As a team, encourage an open-minded attitude. View DISC as a tool to improve understanding and collaboration rather than a means to stereotype or judge each other.

2. The Art of Synergistic Communication

Purpose: Our aim here is to illuminate your style of conveying ideas while gaining a profound understanding of your colleagues' communication preferences. By stepping into this realm, you cultivate a deeper level of empathy and strengthen your interpersonal relationships, both within and outside your team.

Instructions:

1. Kick off the exercise by separating your team into pairs. Give each pair a sheet of paper split into two sections titled "What I Cherish" and "What Irks Me."

2. Encourage each pair to take turns laying bare their unique communication style and preferences. Stimulate this dialogue with thought-provoking prompts like, "Can you share an instance when your communication style helped resolve a conflict?" or "How does your DISC style influence how you express your thoughts?"

3. Next, ask them to identify common ground and differences in their communication styles. You might ask, "What surprised you about your partner's preferences?" or "How do your styles complement each other?"

4. Gather the pairs back into the group's fold. Invite volunteers to shed light on their newfound insights. This leads to greater understanding and mutual respect for team communication styles.

5. Steer the conversation to this pivotal question: "How does knowledge of our diverse styles and preferences empower us to refine communication and enhance collaboration?"

Big Idea: This communication exercise invites you to reflect on your preferences and tune into your colleagues, cultivating an environment of adaptability and mutual respect.

Outcome: Armed with a newfound self-awareness and understanding of each other's communication styles, your team is better equipped to navigate the choppy seas of collaboration. This exercise lays the foundation for a harmonious workplace environment where differences are celebrated and communication is seamless.

Tailoring: This exercise can be finetuned to suit your team's needs. It serves as an engaging icebreaker and a potent tool for refining existing collaboration channels, setting the stage for open communication.

Team Q&A: Below are five potential questions a facilitator might expect to encounter while leading this exercise, along with helpful answers for each:

Question 1: How does the DISC model impact the way we communicate?

Answer 1: It can significantly influence your communication style by revealing the styles of others, and even yourself. For example:

- People with a Dominance (D) style tend to be direct and concise, preferring to get to the point quickly.

- Individuals with an Influence (I) style might be more expressive and enthusiastic in their communication. They often enjoying storytelling, for example.

- People with a Steadiness (S) style are more patient and thoughtful. They prefer collaborative conversations.

- Those with a Conscientiousness (C) style tend to value accuracy, preferring detailed, analytical discussions.

By understanding your DISC style and those of your colleagues, you can tailor your communication for better understanding and collaboration.

Question 2: Is one communication style better than another?

Answer 2: No, there isn't a "better" or "worse" communication style. Every style has its strengths and potential areas for improvement. What matters is understanding each other's styles and preferences. It's about learning how to communicate effectively within a diverse mix. The purpose of this exercise isn't to rank or judge communication styles but to appreciate the richness each brings to team dynamics.

Question 3: How do we handle conflict that arises from different communication styles?

Answer 3: Understanding and respecting different communication styles is the key to resolving conflict. When styles clash, it's crucial to acknowledge your differences and adjust your communication style accordingly. For instance:

- If a D-style person finds a discussion too detailed and lengthy, a C-style communicator could attempt to be more concise, summarizing the main points for clarity.

- If an I-style person feels that their ideas are being brushed over due to their tendency to express thoughts enthusiastically and rapidly, an S-style team member could patiently listen and acknowledge their points to help them feel valued and heard.

It isn't about changing who you are but adapting your style to enhance communication and harmony.

Question 4: What if my communication preferences change over time?

Answer 4: It's entirely normal for those preferences to evolve. As you gain experience and encounter different scenarios, your style might organically shift. That's why it's helpful to revisit exercises like this occasionally, keeping you in tune with each other's current communication styles and preferences to continue communicating effectively.

Question 5: How can we use our understanding of different communication styles to improve collaboration?

Answer 5: A deeper understanding of each other's communication styles helps you adapt your communication to suit your colleagues' preferences, reducing misunderstandings and promoting clear, more effective interactions. For example:

- Knowing that a D-style colleague values decisiveness and brevity, you aim to be direct and concise in your communication.

- If you're collaborating with an S-style teammate who typically prefers a calm, supportive environment, you ensure that your interactions are respectful and patient, and that you involve active listening.

- If you know that a C-style colleague values detailed, precise information, you provide specific details when collaborating on a project.

- Knowing that an I-style teammate thrives in a more social, enthusiastic setting helps you create a more engaging work environment.

You play to each other's strengths and preferences to boost team synergy.

3. Scrutinizing the Spectrum of Leadership Styles

Purpose: This exercise aims to unveil leadership styles, decipher their strengths and weaknesses, and explore their compatibility with your personality type.

Instructions:

1. Initiate the activity by splitting the group into smaller teams. Assign each team a distinct leadership descriptor, such as directive, affiliative, coaching, democratic, or visionary.

2. Endow each team with a palette of information describing their assigned leadership descriptor. Link it to their DISC profile and encourage them to dissect its characteristics and strengths. Ask them, "How do the D, I, S, and C styles

manifest in this leadership descriptor?" or "How can this descriptor's strengths be leveraged in a team setting?"

3. Challenge each team to step into the shoes of their assigned leadership descriptor. Craft a skit or scenario that brings it to life. This is a fun and engaging way to depict the abstract concepts of leadership.

4. Once teams have enacted their engaging skits, converge for a collective debrief. Facilitate a discussion regarding the diverse leadership descriptors and explore how each can be harnessed effectively in varying situations.

Big Idea: This exercise peels back the layers of leadership, giving you a vivid understanding of how different modes align with DISC personality styles. This helps you spot the strengths and weaknesses of each mode to facilitate a broader perspective on leadership.

Outcome: Through this engaging activity, you gain insight into various leadership modes and their alignment with DISC personality styles. From here on out, you'll be equipped with the tools to adapt your leadership mode to any situation.

Team Collaboration: More than just exploring leadership styles, this activity encourages individuals to collectively create skits, share ideas, and understand diverse perspectives. By immersing yourself in this activity, you nurture a vibrant sense of camaraderie and hone your collaborative skills, enhancing overall team synergy.

Team Q&A: Below are five potential questions facilitators should expect while leading this exercise, along with a few helpful answers for each:

Question 1: What's the significance of understanding different leadership modes?

Answer 1: For one, it aids in self-awareness, helping you to better understand your approach to leadership and how it aligns with your DISC profile. Secondly, it facilitates a deeper comprehension of the leadership modes of others, promoting empathy and effective communication within teams. Lastly, having a broad understanding of leadership modes allows you to adapt your approach based on the situation or team's needs.

Question 2: Is one leadership mode better than another?

Answer 2: No "better" or "worse" leadership mode exists. Each one has unique strengths and potential weaknesses, with some being more effective in different situations. For instance, a directive leadership mode may be appropriate in a crisis, while a democratic style might be effective when brainstorming ideas for new projects. The goal of this exercise isn't to rank modes but to understand and appreciate diverse approaches.

Question 3: How do DISC styles relate to the different leadership modes?

Answer 3: DISC styles offer insight into one's preferred leadership mode. For instance:

- An individual with a D style might gravitate toward directive or visionary leadership, given their decisive and goal-oriented nature.

- Conversely, someone with an I style who values interaction and collaboration might resonate with a more democratic or affiliative mode.

- Similarly, an S style might align with affiliative or coaching modes.

- And C styles may align with directive or democratic modes, owing to their analytical and systematic approach.

DISC styles aren't a definitive indicator of one's leadership mode but rather a tool to gain self-insight and help you to understand others.

Question 4: What if a team member identifies with a different leadership mode than their DISC style suggests?

Answer 4: That's completely okay. While DISC styles provide helpful insight, they're not absolute. Individuals can identify with a leadership mode that doesn't typically align with their DISC style. This exercise aims to encourage exploration and self-discovery, not to box anyone into a particular mode. It's about understanding the array of leadership modes and appreciating the strengths each brings to the table.

Question 5: How can we apply the insights gained from this exercise to our work lives?

Answer 5: The insights garnered from this activity are instrumental to team dynamics. By understanding each leadership mode's strengths and potential weaknesses, team members can adapt their approach to suit various situations. For instance, if a team member leans toward a coaching leadership mode, they can leverage this strength to mentor and guide others. Conversely, understanding that a team leader prefers a directive mode helps you match their decision-making approach. These insights refine team interaction, collaboration, and productivity.

4. Embarking on the Personality Treasure Hunt

Purpose: Set sail on a journey of self-discovery and mutual understanding with the Personality Treasure Hunt. Identify and celebrate the unique traits of your DISC profile with this fun-filled, interactive activity while also appreciating team diversity.

Instructions:

1. Form small explorer teams of three to four participants.

2. Give each group a map, with DISC styles shown at one end and treasure circles listing personality traits or characteristics at the other. Include traits like "detail-oriented," "innovative," "team player," "analytical," and more.

3. Set your teams on an intellectual journey to match each personality trait with one of the four DISC styles: Dominance, Influence, Steadiness, and Conscientiousness. For instance, they may correlate "assertiveness" with Dominance and "extroverted" with Influence.

4. Once every group charts their findings, they will then present them to the broader team. Prompt them with questions like, "Why do you think 'detail-oriented' is more associated with Conscientiousness?" and "Why is 'innovative' linked to Influence?"

5. During presentations, stimulate a lively discussion about the reasons behind their correlations to shed light on how different DISC styles embody various personality traits.

6. Finally, steer the participants toward introspection. Ask them to reflect on their personality traits, including which DISC style resonates with them most. Encourage them to share eureka moments and new insights with the group.

Big Idea: The Personality Treasure Hunt immerses you in DISC styles and their associated personality traits. Uncover your unique DISC style while opening the door to self-awareness and personal growth.

Outcome: You'll garner a deeper understanding of the diverse DISC styles and learn how they manifest in team members. Each participant will emerge with a better sense of their strengths and weaknesses.

Team Collaboration: This activity not only enhances self-awareness but also boosts team collaboration. The shared quest to correlate DISC styles with personality traits allows teams to exchange views and understand each other's perspectives, fostering an environment of acceptance and mutual respect.

Team Q&A: Below are five potential questions facilitators should expect to encounter while leading the Personality Treasure Hunt exercise, along with helpful answers for each:

Question 1: How does identifying personality traits relate to our understanding of DISC styles?

Answer 1: The DISC model is a framework for understanding human behavior and personality. Each DISC style—Dominance, Influence, Steadiness, and Conscientiousness—corresponds to specific personality traits. For instance, an outgoing, enthusiastic, and people-oriented person might align with the Influence style. By identifying and associating personality traits with DISC styles, you're better equipped to understand and predict behavior, enhancing communication and team collaboration.

Question 2: Are the personality traits exclusive to one DISC style, or can they be shared across styles?

Answer 2: While certain personality traits may be more prevalent in one DISC style, no characteristic is exclusive to one style. Human behavior is complex and multifaceted, and so individuals exhibit traits from different DISC styles while remaining dominant in one.

- For example, a person might be detail-oriented (often associated with the Conscientiousness style) but also be assertive and direct (traits often linked to the Dominance style).

- They could be patient and reliable (associated with the Steadiness style) while being outgoing and enthusiastic (traits linked to the Influence style).

These multifaceted traits illustrate the complexity of human behavior and the versatility of the DISC framework.

Question 3: What if a participant feels that they don't fit into one DISC style?

Answer 3: That's perfectly normal. People are unique and complex, so while the DISC model provides a useful framework for understanding behavior, it doesn't capture the full spectrum of human personality. It's quite common for someone to identify with traits from multiple DISC styles. The goal of this exercise is to encourage self-discovery and understanding—not to box anyone into a particular style.

Question 4: How can we use the insights gained from this activity in our everyday work lives?

Answer 4: They're valuable in various ways. For starters, understanding your DISC style and its associated traits enhances self-awareness, helping you to recognize your strengths and potential areas for growth. Also, understanding the DISC styles of your colleagues improves communication and collaboration. If a colleague leans toward the Steadiness style, approach them with supportive and thoughtful communication. The insights foster a harmonious and effective working environment.

Question 5: How does this exercise aid in team collaboration?

Answer 5: By working together to match personality traits with DISC styles, team members exchange views and learn more about each other's perspectives, fostering an environment of acceptance and mutual respect. A solid understanding of each other's communication and work styles reduces conflict, improves communication, and enhances team productivity.

5. Exploring Roleplay

Purpose: Embark on a captivating journey of exploration with an exciting roleplaying activity. With this exercise, you dive into the fascinating dynamics of the DISC styles, including how they present themselves in various situations. Your mission is simple—to deepen your understanding of the DISC personality types and improve communication approaches.

Instructions:

1. For your roleplaying adventure, form groups of three participants. Assign each member a role: customer, salesperson, and observer.

2. Arm the customer and the salesperson with a compelling scenario to act out (for example, a curious customer seeking information about a revolutionary product or service). Encourage them to let their natural DISC styles guide their interactions. Ask questions like, "How would a 'Dominance' handle this sales situation?" or "How would a 'Steadiness' respond to this customer's needs?"

3. While the two protagonists bring their scenarios to life, the observer acts as a keen detective, taking note of behaviors and communication styles.

4. After the performance, create a stage for discussion. Encourage the observer to share their findings. Instigate a discussion regarding how each DISC style functioned in the scenario. For example, which communication strategies worked, and which could use some improvement?

Big Idea: This roleplaying exercise highlights how DISC styles interact and behave in different circumstances. It's an engaging way to observe these dynamics firsthand, helping you to appreciate the importance of diverse communication strategies.

Outcome: By stepping into the shoes of those with different DISC styles, you enhance your understanding and learn to adapt your communication style to accommodate various situations. This new perspective enables you to interact more effectively with different personalities, leading to more fruitful outcomes.

Adaptability & Versatility: Mold this activity to suit a variety of scenarios and environments, such as sales training sessions or team-building events. It's especially valuable for those who find communication or conflict resolution challenging. Think of this exercise as a safe space to experience, reflect, and learn. In no time, you'll understand how your behavior affects others, including how slight modifications significantly improve communication and outcomes.

Team Q&A: Below are five potential questions a facilitator might expect to encounter while leading this exercise, along with some helpful answers for each:

Question 1: Who plays the customer, salesperson, and observer?

Answer 1: You can choose them yourselves, if you like. Also, allowing each person to experience all three positions offers a chance to see the scenario from different perspectives. For example, you'll learn to adapt your communication style to other DISC profiles as a salesperson. As a customer, you'll get the chance to see how your DISC profile affects your interactions. As an observer, you'll learn to get comfortable in the cat-bird seat (assessment).

Question 2: As an I type, I found it hard to play a C type. How can I better adapt to other DISC styles?

Answer 2: It's normal to find it challenging to portray an alternate DISC style. It's not about changing your style but about understanding and appreciating other styles. This will help you adjust your approach when communicating with different types. For instance, you might rely on data and details when communicating with C types, even though this isn't your natural style.

Question 3: As a D type, I may have come off as too assertive. How can I adjust this for better communication?

Answer 3: You're naturally direct and assertive, which may annoy or fluster others. Try focusing on the style of others and adjust your approach accordingly. For instance, S and C types often appreciate a more patient, detailed approach. This doesn't mean that you change who you are—you simply try to adapt your style to meet the preferences of others.

Question 4: As the Observer, I missed some key behaviors during the roleplaying exercise. How can I improve my observational skills?

Answer 4: It simply takes practice. As the Observer, keep a keen eye out for behaviors and communication styles associated with DISC profiles. Consider using a checklist or guide to keep track of the various behaviors associated with each profile.

Question 5: How can we use the insights from this roleplaying exercise in our daily interactions?

Answer 5: You can apply the insights to virtually all work areas. Once you understand how different DISC styles interact and communicate, you adjust your communication style to be more effective. The knowledge helps you delegate tasks more effectively if you're a manager. If you're in sales, you can adjust your approach depending on your customer's DISC styles. This understanding significantly enhances teamwork and interpersonal relationships.

6. Exploring Personalities with Bingo

Purpose: Not just regular bingo—DISC Bingo. Who says learning can't be fun? This vibrant activity encourages participants to examine the diverse DISC personality styles in a playful yet profound manner.

Instructions:

1. Craft a colorful bingo card with various traits from each DISC style. Examples could include: "analytical" and "systematic" for Conscientiousness, "outgoing" and "energetic" for Influence, "detail-oriented" and "reliable" for Steadiness, and "independent" and "assertive" for Dominance. Be sure to sprinkle a balanced mix of traits from all four DISC styles.

2. Have each participant customize their bingo card with the traits they feel represent them best. To encourage self-reflection and understanding, ask, "Why do you feel that 'energetic' describes you best?" or "What makes you identify with 'systematic?'"

3. Kickstart the game with enthusiasm. Call out traits from different DISC styles at random. Any participant who has the trait on their bingo card gets the satisfaction of marking it off.

4. Add a spark of competition by celebrating the first participant to get a bingo—a complete row horizontally, vertically, or diagonally.

Big Idea: DISC Bingo isn't just a game. It's a journey of self-discovery and awareness—an entertaining and interactive way to explore the spectrum of DISC styles and their diverse traits, deepening the understanding of yourself and others.

Outcome: As the game progresses, participants learn about the different DISC styles, including how they manifest in various individuals, resulting in a shared understanding of a team's diverse strengths and personalities.

Post-Game Reflections: Afterward, leverage this activity to foster a rich discussion about the different DISC styles. Be sure to ask why participants chose certain traits for their bingo cards. Ask them to share insight into how those traits play out in their professional or personal lives. This reflection period deepens their understanding of the DISC framework and its relevance in everyday interactions.

Team Q&A: Below are five potential questions a facilitator might expect to encounter while leading this exercise, along with helpful answers for each:

Question 1: I'm unsure which traits to put on my bingo card. How do I choose?

Answer 1: Your bingo card should reflect who you are. Consider how you behave in various situations: your work style, interactions with others, and handling stress and decision making. Select the traits that resonate with you the most. There's no right or wrong answer—it's all about self-exploration and understanding.

Question 2: I see myself in traits from all four DISC styles. Is that normal?

Answer 2: Absolutely. Many people identify with traits across the DISC spectrum. Most people are a mixture of styles, with one or two being dominant. This game aims to highlight which styles resonate with you the most.

Question 3: Why is it important to understand DISC styles?

Answer 3: Understanding DISC styles greatly enhances your interactions with others. By understanding your style, you recognize your strengths, preferences, and areas for growth. Knowing the styles of your colleagues helps you improve your communication skills and reduce conflict, promoting a more harmonious and productive working environment.

Question 4: I got a bingo with traits mainly associated with the Steadiness style. What does this mean?

Answer 4: It strongly suggests that you align more with this DISC style. People with a high Steadiness profile are often co-operative and reliable, and they tend to place great importance on harmony and stability. They prefer a steady pace and are patient and good listeners. This may be your primary profile, but your style may vary depending on different factors or circumstances.

Question 5: I won the game, but don't feel like my bingo row accurately represents me. Why?

Answer 5: This is a fun and interactive way to explore DISC styles—not a comprehensive assessment. It's entirely possible that getting a bingo doesn't fully encapsulate your personality. That's okay! Use it as a starting point for self-reflection and deeper exploration of your behavior and communication style. Consider taking a comprehensive DISC assessment for a more in-depth understanding of your style.

7. Self-Awareness: Strengths and Weaknesses

Purpose: Immerse yourself in the rich tapestry of your individuality with the Strengths and Weaknesses exercise, designed to deepen self-awareness. This exercise harmonizes the distinctive DISC framework to illuminate individual strengths and weaknesses.

Instructions:

1. Hand each participant a comprehensive worksheet outlining the four signature DISC styles—Dominance, Influence, Steadiness, and Conscientiousness. Each style should list its unique traits and characteristics. As a facilitator, prime participants with questions like, "As we go through these traits, which ones resonate with you? What feels true about your style?"

2. Invite each person to perform some introspection, identify their primary and secondary DISC styles, and uncover their strengths and weaknesses. You might ask, "How do you see these strengths playing out in your work life?" or "Can you think of a situation where one of these weaknesses may have emerged?"

3. Once they've filled in their worksheets, arrange participants into pairs to discuss their self-reflections. This is a moment of shared learning and empathy, where they offer insight into each other's experiences.

4. Each of the pairs should candidly share their identified DISC styles, strengths, and weaknesses, illuminating these insights by citing examples of how their DISC styles have contributed to or posed challenges in past situations.

5. After facilitating an open discussion in pairs, bring the whole group back together. Stir up a lively conversation around the common themes and insights that've bubbled to the surface. Create an environment where participants can comfortably share revelations about themselves and any future steps they plan to take to magnify their strengths and tackle their weaknesses.

Big Idea: This introspective activity helps participants unearth their strengths and areas for growth based on their DISC profile. With this self-awareness, they can better harness their unique strengths and consciously work on areas of development.

Outcome: After this immersive exercise, individuals leave with a clearer understanding of their DISC style, including the strengths and weaknesses they bring to the table. With an enriched awareness of their capabilities and potential areas for growth, they walk away equipped to use their strengths and improve their weaker traits. The Strengths and Weaknesses activity is more than just an exercise—it's a journey to greater self-awareness.

Team Q&A: Below are five potential questions a facilitator might expect to encounter while leading this exercise, along with helpful answers for each:

Question 1: I identify with characteristics from different DISC styles. How can I pinpoint my primary and secondary styles?

Answer 1: It's perfectly normal to see yourself in multiple DISC styles because most people are a blend of several. Your primary style is typically the one you identify with most intensely and frequently. Your secondary style complements your primary style and is apparent in certain circumstances (though less often). Reflect on which traits dominate in different situations—your usual behavior, your behavior under stress, and your behavior when interacting with others. This should give you a clearer picture of your primary and secondary DISC styles.

Question 2: I've identified my weaknesses, but how can I work on improving them?

Answer 2: Recognizing your weaknesses is the first step toward improvement. Once you've identified areas for growth, you can begin to strategize ways to work on them.

- For example, if you're high in Dominance and overly assertive, you might work on active listening and empathy.

- If you're high in Influence and tend to be too impulsive, striving for more patience and thoughtfulness before making decisions might be beneficial.

- For those with a high Steadiness style who struggle with change and being decisive, actively seeking new experiences and opportunities for change could be a good practice.

- And if you're high in Conscientiousness and struggle with indecision due to wanting specific information, practicing decision making with the available information might be a helpful strategy.

These examples underscore how understanding DISC styles helps us spot areas for personal growth.

Question 3: How do these DISC styles apply to real-life situations?

Answer 3: They provide a lens for understanding your behavior and communication style in various situations. For instance:

- If you're a Steadiness type, you might be calm and composed during stressful situations.

- Dominance types might take charge and lead.

- If you lean toward the Conscientiousness style, you might tackle challenges with a systematic and detail-oriented approach, providing comprehensive solutions.

- If you resonate more with the Influence style, you may employ exceptional interpersonal skills and enthusiasm to encourage others and build morale during tough times.

Understanding these styles helps you to leverage your strengths and navigate challenges more effectively in your personal and professional life.

Question 4: How does knowing our DISC styles help with team collaboration?

Answer 4: When team members understand their styles and those of their colleagues, they communicate more effectively, appreciate diverse viewpoints, and work harmoniously. This leads to a more productive, understanding, and efficient team environment.

Question 5: How accurate is my DISC profile? Can it change over time?

Answer 5: The DISC profile is a valuable tool for understanding one's behavior and communication style—and it simplifies complex human behavior. It's a framework for understanding ourselves and others. That said, it's not definitive or unchangeable. Our behaviors evolve with personal growth, environmental changes, and life experiences. So while your DISC profile provides valuable insight, it's just one of the many tools for understanding your behavior.

8. Charting Your Destiny: Career Mapping

Purpose: Using the Career Mapping exercise as a compass for navigating your professional journey. Whether you're a professional seeking clarity or a manager aiming to amplify your team's potential, this is your guide. The exercise finesses the DISC model to align career paths with personality types.

Instructions:

1. Have each participant take a DISC assessment to unveil their dominant behavioral style. As a facilitator, you could ask, "Are you surprised by your DISC results? What stands out to you about your behavioral style?"

2. Guided by the newfound knowledge of their DISC style, participants should delve into their career dreams and ambitions, pinpointing the vital skills and competencies that turn vision into reality. At this stage, they should be brutally honest about identifying the gaps or areas needing development in their career journey. Encourage participants by saying, "Let's dare to dream big here. Imagine your career five or ten years down the line. What does it look like? What skills have you mastered?"

3. Next, ask participants to channel their reflections into a career map that crystallizes their objectives, requisite skills and competencies, and the strategic steps required to reach their goals. Short- and long-term goals should be on this map, accompanied by specific, actionable steps to achieve them.

4. With individual maps ready, create a nurturing space for participants to share their career aspirations and plans. Facilitate a discussion around how they can lean on each other's strengths and compensate for one another's weaknesses to reach their goals collectively.

Big Idea: This exercise uses the foundation of the DISC framework to facilitate career planning and align one's professional ambitions with one's behavioral style. It helps you create a roadmap that honors your unique personality while helping you achieve career aspirations.

Outcome: The Career Mapping exercise equips participants with a tangible roadmap to their career aspirations, linked intricately to their unique DISC style. A clear understanding of their professional objectives and the steps to achieve them is an empowering takeaway.

Team Q&A: Below are five potential questions a facilitator might encounter while leading this exercise, along with helpful answers for each:

Question 1: How will my DISC style influence my career path?

Answer 1: It provides insight into your strengths, weaknesses, communication style, and approach to problems and challenges—all of which valuable in determining which careers or roles fit your natural inclinations. For example, if you're high in Influence, roles requiring strong interpersonal skills and the ability to motivate others may be a good fit. Likewise, if you're high in Conscientiousness, you may thrive in roles that require attention to detail and a systematic approach.

Question 2: I have ambitious career goals, but my DISC style suggests that I need help to reach them. What should I do?

Answer 2: Your DISC style isn't a limitation—it's a starting point for understanding your behavioral tendencies. If your career goals require skills or behaviors that aren't typically associated with your DISC style, it doesn't mean that those goals are unattainable. It simply means that you might need to exert extra effort. Use your DISC style to understand where to grow and adapt.

Question 3: Can my DISC style change over time, especially as I progress in my career?

Answer 3: While your core DISC style remains relatively stable, your behaviors can evolve and adapt over time due to personal growth, life experiences, and professional development. This is particularly true as you assume new roles and responsibilities. What's important is that you remain aware of these shifts and continually reassess and refine your career map when necessary.

Question 4: What if I'm still unsure about my career goals?

Answer 4: That's perfectly fine. The beauty of the Career Mapping exercise is that it helps you explore possibilities. You don't need to know exactly where you're going—you just need to start thinking about it. Reflect on your DISC style and think about the type of work that energizes you. Consider what you might want to develop further. This process alone provides valuable insight to guide your career journey.

Question 5: Can I use this career map to discuss my career development with my manager?

Answer 5: Absolutely! Sharing your career map with your manager is a great way to initiate dialogue about your career development. It shows that you've considered your strengths and weaknesses, including where you want to be professionally. Plus, it provides a solid foundation for discussing how your manager and organization can support you in achieving your career goals.

9. Harmonizing Differences: Conflict Resolution

Purpose: This exercise dives deep into conflict resolution—with a colorful twist tailored to complement different DISC styles. By enabling participants to know how their DISC profile influences their approach to conflict resolution, this activity encourages mutual understanding and paves the way for more effective conflict-management strategies.

Instructions:

1. First, confirm that each participant has undergone a DISC assessment.

2. Divide participants into small, intimate groups. This sets the stage for an open and nuanced discussion. Provide each

group with a hypothetical conflict scenario, a vibrant backdrop against which they can explore their conflict-resolution styles. As a facilitator, you could ask, "How does this situation resonate with your experience of conflict situations in the past?"

3. Each participant, equipped with insights from their DISC profile, shares their unique conflict-resolution style, explaining how they would navigate the hypothetical conflict scenario. Prompt them by asking, "How does your DISC style influence your approach to resolving conflict?"

4. The crux of the activity unfolds as the group dives into the labyrinth of DISC styles. The goal is to discuss the dynamic interplay between various styles, including how they clash and complement one another. They should also brainstorm strategies to resolve conflict in a way that respects and accommodates everyone's style and needs.

5. Finally, provide participants with a space to reflect on their conflict-resolution styles. Allow them the room to learn how they can flex their style to better collaborate with diverse personalities.

Big Idea: This exercise aims to help participants understand the root of their conflict-resolution style, including how their style aligns with their DISC profile. This cultivates empathy, improves collaboration, and facilitates productive conflict resolution.

Outcome: By the end of the exercise, participants have a profound understanding of their conflict-resolution style as it relates to their DISC style. They're equipped with practical strategies for harmonizing their approach with others' approaches to navigate and resolve conflict effectively. With greater self-awareness and respect for diverse styles, they're better prepared to engage in conflict situations productively and collaboratively.

Team Q&A: Below are five potential questions a facilitator might expect to encounter while leading this exercise, along with helpful answers for each:

Question 1: How does my DISC style influence how I handle conflict?

Answer 1: It provides insight into your behavioral tendencies, including how you handle conflict. For instance:

- If you're high in Dominance, you might be more assertive and direct, tackling issues head-on.

- If you're high in Steadiness, you might prefer to avoid conflict and work toward a consensus.

- Someone with a high Conscientiousness score may approach conflict analytically, carefully evaluating all aspects of a situation before acting.

- Individuals with a high Influence score might use communication and persuasion skills to diffuse conflict and build consensus.

Understanding your style helps you recognize your natural approach to conflict resolution, including the areas you need to develop.

Question 2: What if my approach to conflict resolution clashes with someone else's style?

Answer 2: This is likely to happen in a diverse team, and it's where the value of this exercise lies. By understanding how different DISC styles approach conflict, you learn to empathize with others and adapt your style when necessary. You try to find common ground and develop strategies that respect everyone's needs and preferences.

Question 3: If my style naturally avoids conflict, does that mean I'm disadvantaged?

Answer 3: Not at all. Every DISC style has its strengths and areas for growth. If your style avoids conflict, you likely excel at maintaining harmony and fostering a positive team atmosphere. But there may be times when conflict is necessary to address issues or stimulate change. You should push yourself to engage more directly in these instances.

Question 4: What if I'm dealing with a personal conflict rather than a professional one?

Answer 4: You can resolve personal conflict better with an understanding of DISC. How we handle conflict doesn't change drastically between our personal and professional lives. Recognizing how you and the other party approach conflict based on your DISC styles helps foster understanding and guides resolution.

Question 5: Can we use the knowledge from this exercise in future conflict resolution?

Answer 5: Absolutely—that's the goal. The insights you gain regarding your conflict-resolution style and those of others should serve as a guide for future conflict situations. The more you understand the diverse approaches to conflict, the better equipped you'll be to navigate it in a way that respects everyone's style and promotes constructive outcomes.

10. Unifying Forces: Team Building

Purpose: Participants form intimate teams to tackle team-building challenges. This sheds light on each DISC style's strengths, highlighting the power of diversity while fostering solid bonds within teams.

Instructions:

1. Have team members take a DISC assessment, revealing their unique personality style and serving as the basis for understanding and leveraging their strengths.

2. Encourage the team to huddle and delve into the world of DISC. Ask them to discuss the characteristics and strengths in each personality style, and to question potential challenges or weaknesses. As a facilitator, you might ask, "How do you feel your DISC style enhances your contribution to the team?"

3. It's time to put theory into practice. Invite the team to participate in an activity that demands cooperation and seamless communication to capitalize on each member's strengths. Whether a problematic task or a creative project, this activity should resonate with the team and encourage them to harness their diverse skill sets.

4. Afterward, gather your team for a reflective debrief. Discuss their experience and focus on how they collaborated and navigated the task. Ask them questions like, "Can you recall a moment when you felt your DISC style was an asset?" and "Were there instances where you felt challenged due to your DISC style?" Encourage them to identify moments of success and areas for improvement.

5. Together, chart a roadmap for future teamwork. This action plan should draw upon their newfound understanding of each other's DISC styles and identify strategies to enhance team performance. This could involve assigning roles catering to each member's strengths or developing strategies to navigate future conflict.

Big Idea: The DISC-focused Team Building illuminates each member's unique personality style and the potential they bring to the team. It's a master class in embracing diversity and transforming it into a powerful force for team success.

Outcome: Through this enlightening exercise, your team can better understand each other's strengths and how to leverage them cooperatively for success. They gain insight into their DISC styles, improving collaboration and communication. With an action plan, they're ready to take their teamwork to new heights, leading to more successful projects and a harmonious working environment.

Team Q&A: Below are five potential questions a facilitator might expect to encounter while conducting this exercise, along with helpful answers for each:

Question 1: How can knowing my team members' DISC styles improve our teamwork?

Answer 1: It helps you grasp how your teammates prefer to work, communicate, and make decisions. For instance:

- A D-style individual might prefer direct, concise communication.

- I-style people thrive in social situations and may favor more informal discussions.

- An S-style person likely values harmony and cooperation. They may appreciate a more collaborative decision-making approach.

- C-style people, who value accuracy and detail, prefer comprehensive information and adequate time to make critical decisions.

Understanding these preferences helps you adapt your approach to communicating and collaborating more effectively, leading to improved teamwork skills.

Question 2: I'm unsure of how my DISC style contributes to the team. Can you explain it to me?

Answer 2: Absolutely. Each DISC style comes with a unique set of strengths that contribute to a team. D-style people are decisive and results-oriented. I-style individuals are great at inspiring others and creating a positive atmosphere. S-style people are reliable and supportive—the glue that keeps a team together. C-style individuals are thorough, accurate, and keen on detail. Identifying your style and strengths helps you understand the role you play in your team.

Question 3: How can we resolve a conflict if our DISC styles clash?

Answer 3: It's not so much "clashing" as it is "differing." That's an important perspective to keep in mind. It takes understanding and respect. When you know someone's DISC style, you can see their perspective more clearly and empathize with their approach, even if it differs from yours. Rather than viewing these differences as a source of conflict, you'll see them as an opportunity to learn and grow. With mutual respect and open communication, you navigate these differences and find a middle ground that works for everyone.

Question 4: I'm the only one with a particular DISC style in the team. Is this a disadvantage?

Answer 4: Quite the opposite. Your unique DISC style is an asset to your team, since each style brings different strengths to the table. Diversity enhances team performance by offering a wide range of skills, perspectives, and approaches to problem solving. Embrace your unique style and look for ways to harness your strengths to benefit the team.

Question 5: Our team is remote. Can we still effectively implement this exercise?

Answer 5: Yes, with a little more technological finesse. Other than that, it's no different. Discuss and reflect over video platforms as you would in-person. Even remotely, your team will gain valuable insight into each other's DISC styles to enhance collaboration and communication.

11. Uplifting Each Other: Positive Reinforcement

Purpose: Participants engage in close-knit groups to brainstorm and generate effective strategies for positively acknowledging and reinforcing various personality types within their workspace.

Instructions:

1. Give each team member a detailed worksheet delineating the various DISC styles and their corresponding traits. This serves as a foundation for discussion and feedback.

2. Prompt each participant to reflect on their team members. Identify three strikingly positive traits in everyone's DISC style. Focusing on attributes that positively contribute to team dynamics is crucial. As a facilitator, you could ask, "What are the key strengths of your team members that resonate with their DISC style?"

3. Now comes the exciting part—inviting each participant to share their feedback with the group. Ensure that it's genuine, precise, and focused more on actions and behaviors than personality traits. For instance:

    - A team member with a Dominance (D) style could be commended for their inspiring leadership skills or quick, decisive action in the face of challenges.

    - Those exhibiting an Influential (I) style might receive praise for their exceptional communication skills or the energy and enthusiasm they bring to the team.

- Individuals with a Steadiness (S) style could be recognized for their reliability and the calming, stabilizing presence they contribute, even in turbulent times.

- Those showcasing a Conscientiousness (C) style might be lauded for their meticulous attention to detail, analytical thinking, and commitment to maintaining high standards.

Big Idea: This exercise is designed to cultivate a culture of positivity, appreciation, and mutual respect within teams. It's an opportunity to highlight each team member's strengths and talents and foster a sense of unity and mutual support. It encourages self-awareness among participants, helping them understand their DISC style better and discover how they can contribute to the team.

Outcome: At the end of this exercise, participants should have a profound appreciation for each other's strengths and a clear understanding of how these strengths contribute to team success. Bonds are strengthened, and members come away feeling valued and acknowledged. This exercise enhances team performance, generating a positive work environment where everyone understands, appreciates, and positively reinforces each other's unique DISC style.

Team Q&A: Below are five potential questions a facilitator might expect to encounter while conducting this exercise, along with helpful answers for each:

Question 1: How does positive reinforcement impact team performance?

Answer 1: Positive reinforcement acknowledges the strengths of individuals, which motivates them to perform well. It also cultivates a positive work environment, enhancing job satisfaction, productivity, and overall team performance. By reinforcing each other's unique DISC style, your team acknowledges the value of diversity and promotes a culture where everyone feels seen and appreciated.

Question 2: I'm unsure if my positive traits align with my DISC style. Can you help me understand?

Answer 2: Absolutely. Each DISC style comes with its own set of positive traits, so you need to focus specifically on those traits and see if they line up.

- If you're a D-style individual, your strengths likely lie in your ability to lead, make decisions, and tackle challenges head-on.

- I-style people often bring enthusiasm, optimism, and excellent interpersonal skills to the team.

- S-style individuals are typically cooperative, reliable, and great listeners.

- C-style people are generally known for their precision, analytical skills, and adherence to standards.

Question 3: How can we continue to practice positive reinforcement outside of this exercise?

Answer 3: Try simple acts like acknowledging a team member's good work, sending appreciative emails, and providing supportive feedback. Try to be specific, immediate, and sincere to generate the most significant impact.

Question 4: I'm afraid that focusing on positive traits might make us overlook areas that need improvement. How do we balance this?

Answer 4: Positive reinforcement isn't about ignoring areas for improvement—it's about highlighting strengths to encourage more positive behavior. Constructive feedback regarding areas for development is still crucial. The key is to provide balanced feedback—acknowledging strengths while guiding improvement. Understanding your team members' DISC styles helps you tailor your input effectively.

Question 5: What if my positive reinforcement doesn't align with a team member's DISC style?

Answer 5: Focus more clearly on the individual's DISC style and then work on re-tailoring your reinforcement. Be creative. For example:

- D-style individuals may prefer public recognition for their achievements, which showcases their accomplishments and determination.

- I-style people, generally known for their outgoing and enthusiastic nature, might appreciate a lively celebration or the opportunity to share their success story with the team.

- S-style individuals, often quieter and more reserved, might prefer discrete, one-on-one acknowledgment since they appreciate a genuine and personalized touch.

- C-style team members, who tend to be analytical and detail-oriented, value thorough feedback regarding the quality and precision of their work.

If you're still unsure, ask a team member about their preferences. Understanding and respecting each other's DISC styles ensures that positive reinforcement remains meaningful and effective.

12. Exploring Personality Profiles

Purpose: Participants delve into their DISC personalities, initiating conversations on striking similarities and intriguing differences between styles. This, in turn, enhances team self-awareness.

Instructions:

1. Ensure that each team member has their DISC profile at hand. This will act as a compass throughout the exercise.

2. Next, it's time for a bit of matchmaking! Divide your team into pairs or small clusters. Ask them to compare and contrast their DISC profiles to identify parallels and variances in their personality types. As a facilitator, you might ask, "What similarities and differences do you see in your DISC styles? How might these impact your communication and collaboration strategies?"

3. Afterward, encourage each pair or group to reflect on how their unique personalities influence how they communicate and work together. The objective is to identify strategies that make collaboration smooth and efficient.

4. Gather everyone and initiate a vibrant discussion where each group shares their insights. Stimulate conversations around leveraging their newfound understanding to enhance communication, teamwork, and overall team dynamics.

Big Idea: This exercise aims to heighten team self-awareness and mutual understanding. By dissecting and discussing individual DISC profiles, team members gain a better grasp of their communication styles. This shared understanding significantly boosts team cohesion and interpersonal communication.

Outcome: Upon concluding this exercise, your team should buzz with fresh insights into their individual and collective DISC profiles. They emerge with a heightened sense of self-awareness, a better understanding of team dynamics, and tangible strategies for improving communication and collaboration. The ultimate reward? A more harmonious and productive team that appreciates and leverages their unique DISC styles.

Team Q&A: Below are five potential questions a facilitator might expect to encounter while conducting this exercise, along with helpful answers for each:

Question 1: How does understanding my DISC profile help improve my work performance?

Answer 1: It significantly enhances your self-awareness by providing insight into your work style, communication approach, and response to conflict. These insights enable you to refine your approach to collaboration, communication, and problem solving, ultimately improving your work performance. For instance:

- If you have a Dominance (D) style, you might be great at decision making, but your patience and listening skills could use a little work.

- If your profile leans toward an Influence (I) style, you're probably highly social and enthusiastic, and you may need to work on your focus and consistency.

- For a Steadiness (S) style, although you might be a great team player and reliable colleague, you could benefit from boosting your assertiveness during conflict.

- If your profile aligns with the Conscientiousness (C) style, attention to small details and analytical thinking are common strengths. You might work on being more adaptable and comfortable in less structured environments.

Question 2: How does understanding similarities and differences in DISC profiles impact team performance?

Answer 2: It fosters mutual respect and understanding, which improves team cohesion. You come to appreciate the unique contributions of each team member and are better equipped to navigate potential conflicts. For instance, if you're an I-style individual working with a C-style teammate, you'll understand the importance of providing them with detailed information and plenty of time for analysis, which may not be your usual approach.

Question 3: What if my DISC profile drastically differs from my team's predominant style?

Answer 3: Diversity in styles is a plus, since each style brings a unique set of strengths to a team. If your DISC profile differs from your team's predominant style, you offer a perspective and set of skills that complement your teammates'. For instance, if you're an S-style individual in a team of D-style teammates, your listening ability and emphasis on teamwork can balance team dynamics.

Question 4: How can two team members work together effectively if they have conflicting DISC styles?

Answer 4: Recognizing and understanding differences in DISC styles is the first step to working together effectively, allowing team members to adapt their communication and collaboration strategies to accommodate each other's styles.

- For instance, a D-style individual, generally direct and decisive, can be more patient and receptive when interacting with an S-style person, who may be more reserved, preferring stability and consensus.

- An I-style individual (typically enthusiastic and sociable) could be mindful of providing more structured and detailed communication when collaborating with a C-style colleague who usually values precision and analytical information.

- A C-style person, who tends to be methodical and detail-oriented, can strive to be more flexible and open to spontaneous discussions when working with an I-style teammate, generally known for their creativity and outgoing nature.

Understanding these dynamics and adapting accordingly is crucial for effective teamwork.

Question 5: How can we apply the insights from this exercise to everyday team interactions?

Answer 5: Be mindful of your team members' DISC styles when communicating, delegating tasks, and resolving conflicts. Oftentimes, flexing your style to accommodate others is necessary. Eventually, this understanding and flexibility leads to strengthened communication, better collaboration, and a more cohesive team.

13. Unlocking Effective Communication

Purpose: The goal here is to optimize communication strategies that resonate with different personality types effectively. Participants undertake a thorough communication assessment and engage in group discussions about their findings.

Instructions:

1. After each participant is partnered up, have them enter a state of introspection. Give them a few quiet moments to mull over their communication styles, as well as their verbal strengths and areas that require improvement. Engage them by asking questions like, "In which areas of communication do you feel powerful? Where do you face challenges?"

2. Once everyone forms an opinion on their communication styles, invite them to share their insights with their partner or the group.

3. The next phase is an exchange of words—literally! Each participant takes turns playing the role of the speaker while their partner assumes the role of listener. As a speaker, they exercise their communication skills, while the listener pays close attention to the speaker's style, choice of words, tone, and body language. As the facilitator, guide them with prompts like "Focus on the speaker's use of words. Are they clear and concise? Do they use body language effectively?"

4. After the speaker finishes, it's time for feedback. The listener shares broad observations regarding the speaker's effective technique and areas for growth.

5. Switch roles and repeat the process. Give everyone a chance to experience both parts, and feel free to run several rounds of the exercise. Focus on varying facets of their communication style each time.

Big Idea: This exercise develops a heightened awareness of communication style and its impact on others. Constructive feedback is a mirror, reflecting verbal strengths and potential blind spots, which empowers employees to craft a more refined communication style.

Outcome: Emerging from this activity, participants possess a clearer picture of their communication style, strengths, and aspects that require polishing. They also can better understand how their DISC profile influences their communication style. Equipped with these insights, they're better positioned to hone their communication skills, ensuring that they resonate effectively across diverse personality types.

Team Q&A: Below are five potential questions a facilitator might expect to encounter while conducting this exercise, along with helpful answers for each:

Question 1: How does understanding my DISC profile help improve my communication skills?

Answer 1: It provides insight into your natural communication style and preferences. For instance:

- If you're high in Dominance, you may favor direct, concise communication and excel in decision making. However, you might need to work on active listening and empathy to build better connections with your team.

- If your style leans toward Influence, you're likely comfortable with open, enthusiastic communication and are probably excellent at persuading others. You might need to concentrate on being more concise and attentive to details.

- As a Steadiness type, you generally value cooperation and stability in communication but could benefit from asserting your needs and ideas more clearly.

- If you have a high Conscientiousness style, you likely excel at delivering detailed, analytical information, but perhaps could work on being more flexible and tolerant in less structured discussions.

By understanding these tendencies, you effectively enhance your strengths and address your weaknesses to improve communication.

Question 2: What if the feedback I receive about my communication style is harsh or unexpected?

Answer 2: Receiving feedback can be a challenging experience, mainly if it's out of the blue or seems a bit severe. But the purpose of this exercise is to help you improve, so encourage the person giving you feedback to be constructive and specific. Take their observations (even if seemingly harsh) as an opportunity to learn and grow, not as personal criticism. For example, if your communication style is largely empathetic and understanding, you might work on being more direct and concise.

Question 3: How can I adjust my communication style to better interact with different DISC styles?

Answer 3: You achieve this by clearly understanding the different DISC styles—and then modifying your communication approach. For example:

- D-style individuals appreciate brief, to-the-point communication.

- I-styles respond to enthusiastic, engaging interactions.

- S-styles value supportive, collaborative language.

- C-styles prefer detailed, logical information.

With these clear styles in mind, tailor your communication accordingly to better engage with your teammates.

Question 4: Can my DISC style change? If so, how will it affect my communication skills?

Answer 4: While your core DISC style tends to remain consistent, it can change depending on your environment and role. For example, an S-style person promoted to a leadership role might display more D-style characteristics over time. It's important to regularly reassess your DISC style and its impact on your communication style as your personal and professional circumstances evolve.

Question 5: How will this exercise help improve team communication and dynamics?

Answer 5: By gaining insight into each other's communication styles, team members understand and respond to one another better. This effective and harmonious communication reduces misunderstanding and conflict, and it nurtures a more supportive and efficient team environment.

14. Mastering Decision Making

Purpose: With this exercise, we're brainstorming collective strategies that play to each personality type's strengths to foster harmonious and effective decision making. Participants collaborate in compact teams and delve into the intriguing decision-making patterns of different personality types (DISC styles).

Instructions:

1. Ensure that each participant has taken the DISC assessment and has identified their dominant behavioral style. This serves as a roadmap for navigating the exercise.

2. Set the tone by elucidating and emphasizing the integral role of quality decisions in personal and professional scenarios. You might pose questions like, "Can anyone share a time when they made a decision that significantly impacted a project or their team?"

3. Divide your participants into compact think tanks of three to four people. Size matters! Keeping groups small encourages active participation from all members.

4. Stoke their thought processes by presenting each team with a scenario requiring decision-making prowess. This could be a complex business problem, a personal dilemma to untangle, or a team obstacle to conquer.

5. Next, spotlight their DISC profiles. Invite each team member to articulate their preferred decision-making style per their profile.

6. Facilitate a vibrant discussion within each team based on their decision-making styles. Encourage them to explore how to harness and combine their strengths to produce optimal outcomes.

7. Each team presentation should illustrate their decision-making journey and emphasize how their DISC profiles influence their approach.

8. Conclude the exercise by spearheading a group dialogue to compare and contrast each team's different decision-making styles and methodologies.

Big Idea: The Mastering Decision Making activity centers around pinpointing individual decision-making patterns, including how they relate to DISC profiles. This insight, combined with understanding others' styles, enables participants to better navigate group decisions.

Outcome: Participants should better understand their decision-making tendencies and the unique strengths and challenges associated with their DISC profiles. This enhanced awareness promotes improved collaboration and communication within teams, leading to cohesive decision making and bolstering overall team performance.

Team Q&A: Below are five potential questions a facilitator might expect to encounter while conducting this exercise, along with helpful answers for each:

Question 1: How does my DISC profile influence my decision-making style?

Answer 1: Your DISC profile identifies traits that bear on decision making. For example:

- If you have a high Dominance (D) style, you might make decisions quickly and confidently, focusing on solutions and results.

- People with a high Influence (I) style might make decisions based on personal feelings and their impact on relationships.

- Steadiness (S) types often prefer collaborative decision making, considering the feelings and input of others.

- Conscientiousness (C) types tend to be analytical and thorough in their decision making, relying on data and information to feel comfortable with their choices.

Question 2: What if my decision-making style clashes with a teammate's?

Answer 2: You turn the "clash" into a dance. It's natural to encounter different decision-making styles in teams, but understanding your DISC profile and the profiles of your teammates helps you navigate and *use* these differences. For instance, if you're a D-style person and your teammate is an S style, recognizing that they require more time and input from others makes you more patient and inclusive in the decision-making process.

Question 3: What if I'm part of a team where all members share the same DISC style? Won't our decision-making process be one-sided?

Answer 3: Perhaps a bit less *interesting*, but not necessarily one-sided. While having a team with similar DISC styles comprises certain shared tendencies, members still often have different perspectives and ideas. Also, even when a team has a uniform style, it's beneficial to be aware of the potential biases of your DISC style and consciously seek to incorporate diverse views and partnerships.

Question 4: How will this exercise help improve our team's decision-making process?

Answer 4: It highlights the various styles within your team, identifying each member's strengths and weaknesses, and promoting a balanced and inclusive decision-making strategy. For example, knowing that your C-style teammate prefers data-driven decisions, you might make a point to include relevant data in team discussions.

Question 5: How can we ensure that every team member's decision-making style is acknowledged and valued?

Answer 5: The key is to foster an environment of mutual respect and open communication, and to encourage each team member to understand and appreciate different decision-making styles. During team discussions, ensure that everyone gets an opportunity to contribute and have their input genuinely considered. The goal isn't to dominate or compromise but to collaborate effectively, leveraging each person's strengths.

15. Navigating Cultural Diversity

Purpose: The goal of this exercise is to help team members understand and appreciate the role that different cultural perspectives and communication styles play in nurturing a harmonious work environment. Teams embark on a journey to explore how different personality types approach cultural diversity within workplace settings.

Instructions:

1. Divide participants into small groups, ensuring that each team embodies a mix of DISC profiles. The diverse composition of each group better mirrors real-life work scenarios and enhances the richness of discussions.

2. Assign each team a cultural scenario to ponder. This could revolve around distinct communication methods, traditional customs, fundamental values, or deep-seated beliefs.

3. Have each team tap into their knowledge of DISC profiles and understanding of cultural sensitivity. Their task is to brainstorm effective strategies for seamless communication

and collaboration with individuals from assigned cultures. Encourage them to consider how the elements of their assigned culture shape communication, including how they can adapt their DISC styles in response.

4. After brainstorming, teams reconvene with the larger group and present their strategies and insight. As they share their findings, ensure that every voice is heard to facilitate a diverse exchange of perspectives.

5. As a facilitator, guide group discussions post-presentation and delve into the impact of varied cultural scenarios regarding communication dynamics and interpersonal relationships. Discuss the power of DISC profiles in understanding and bridging gaps with individuals from various cultural backgrounds.

Big Idea: The Cultural Diversity exercise harnesses DISC profiles to facilitate understanding and empathy for various cultures. Participants gain a deeper awareness of their biases and behaviors by focusing on the roles of their personality types while navigating cultural diversity. This accelerates personal growth and improves multicultural communication skills.

Outcome: Participants emerge with an enhanced capacity for empathy, cultural awareness, and effective communication. These newfound skills help build solid and understanding relationships within teams, paving the way for a more inclusive and culturally diverse work environment. With diversity acknowledged and celebrated, a sense of unity and shared understanding galvanizes teams.

Team Q&A: Below are five potential questions a facilitator might expect to encounter while conducting this exercise, along with helpful answers for each:

Question 1: How does my DISC profile affect how I approach cultural diversity?

Answer 1: Your profile reflects your behavioral tendencies, which influence your interactions with different cultures.

- If you're a high Dominance (D) type, you might focus on direct and efficient communication, which can clash with cultures that value indirect or subtle ways of expressing thoughts.

- If you're an Influence (I) style, you might thrive in open, enthusiastic, and people-oriented situations, which could be overwhelming to individuals from cultures that value more reserved and introspective communication styles.

- If you lean toward the Steadiness (S) style, you may emphasize harmony, patience, and cooperation, which could be misinterpreted by cultures that value assertiveness and quick decision making.

- As a high Conscientiousness (C) type, your tendency for precision, logic, and detail-oriented communication could come across as overly analytical or distant to cultures that favor personal connection and emotional expressiveness.

Understanding these tendencies allows you to adjust your approach to communicate more effectively across cultures.

Question 2: What if I'm unfamiliar with the culture assigned to my team?

Answer 2: That's okay! This exercise helps you learn about and consider different cultures. The key is approaching this task with an open mind and a willingness to learn, so use this opportunity to research and discuss with your team. Remember, the diversity of your team's DISC profiles will contribute to various perspectives.

Question 3: How can I better adapt my communication style to different cultural norms?

Answer 3: The first step is awareness—understanding your communication style as reflected in your DISC profile and learning about the communication norms of the culture you're interacting with. From here, you need flexibility and empathy. For example:

- Suppose you have a high Influence (I) style and enjoy friendly, enthusiastic communication, but you're interacting with a culture that values formality and restraint. You might temper your exuberance and prioritize respect for cultural norms.

- If you have a high Dominance (D) style and tend to communicate directly and decisively but you're interacting with a culture that values indirect communication and consensus building, soften your approach and show more patience with the decision-making process.

- If you have a high Steadiness (S) style and typically seek harmony and stability but engage with a culture that values innovation and risk taking, try demonstrating openness to new ideas and adaptability to change.

- If you're high in Conscientiousness (C) and prefer precise, analytical communication but you're dealing with a culture that favors emotional expressiveness and personal relationships, incorporate personal anecdotes and expressive language when communicating.

In every case, you must balance your natural communication style with empathy and respect for the cultural norms of those you're interacting with.

Question 4: Our team struggled with some cultural misunderstandings during this exercise. How can we avoid such incidents in the future?

Answer 4: Experiencing such misunderstandings indicates areas for learning and growth. To prevent such future incidents, use these misunderstandings as a starting point for further discussion. Learn more about the cultures you struggle to understand and consider how your DISC profiles might influence perceptions. Emphasize open dialogue, empathy, and knowledge in all your interactions.

Question 5: How does understanding our DISC profiles create a more culturally diverse work environment?

Answer 5: DISC profiles help you understand your communication style and the styles of others, including their preferences and behaviors. This enhances empathy and understanding among team members from different cultural backgrounds. For example, suppose a team member from a high-context culture (preferring indirect communication) feels misunderstood. Adapting your communication style to suit their preferences will lead to compelling and harmonious interactions.

16. Mastering Emotion Management

Purpose: With this exercise, we're encouraging individuals to delve into their emotional reservoirs to cultivate self-awareness and find ways to efficiently manage their emotions—all through the lens of their DISC personality style.

Instructions:

1. Assemble participants into compact groups. Your first mission is to help everyone pinpoint emotional triggers—instances, behaviors, or circumstances that spark emotional reaction. As the facilitator, consider prompts like "Reflect on moments when you felt a strong emotional reaction. What were the circumstances? Who was involved? What feelings did those situations evoke in you?"

2. Next, it's time to examine the emotional response to these triggers—the intensity, longevity, and effect of participants' feelings. A facilitator prompt might be, "How would you rate the intensity of your feelings on a scale from 1-10? How long do these emotions usually persist? How does this emotional response impact your behavior and decision making?"

3. Each person will now probe the origin of their emotional triggers, assessing whether they're tethered to specific individuals and situations or rooted in personal beliefs. An excellent facilitator prompt could be, "What or who appears to be the common denominator in these emotionally charged instances? Do you notice any patterns?"

4. Curate an emotion management strategy and craft a personalized blueprint to manage emotional responses. This could involve conscious breathing, constructive self-talk, or taking a break from triggering situations. A facilitator prompt might be, "What calming strategies can you employ when faced with these triggers? How can you harness your DISC style strengths to manage emotional responses?"

5. Now it's time to put the tailored plan into action, with everyone dedicating time to practice and refine it, which arms them with the competence to tackle emotional responses adeptly. An effective facilitator prompt could be, "Commit to practicing your emotion management strategy and make adjustments as necessary. Remember, progress over perfection is the goal."

Big Idea: This exercise, rooted in the DISC framework, enhances emotional self-awareness and arms participants with practical strategies to manage emotions. Emotional intelligence enhances interpersonal communication, healthier relationships, and well-being.

Outcome: Upon completing this journey, participants can better understand their emotional triggers and are equipped with a practical toolkit to manage their emotional responses—paving the way for productive communication, healthier relationships, and a heightened sense of well-being.

Team Q&A: Below are five potential questions a facilitator might expect to encounter while conducting this exercise, along with helpful answers for each:

Question 1: How does my DISC profile influence my emotional triggers?

Answer 1: Your DISC profile outlines your dominant behavioral tendencies, which influence your emotional triggers. For example:

- A person with a Dominance (D) style might be easily frustrated when they feel that their autonomy is threatened or when decisions are made without their input.

- Individuals with an Influence (I) style generally become upset if they feel ignored or their ideas aren't acknowledged, given their preference for social recognition and interaction.

- A person with a Steadiness (S) style might feel distressed if pushed into sudden changes or high-pressure situations, given their preference for stability and harmony.

- An individual with a Conscientiousness (C) style might feel anxious if they lack detailed information or their work is criticized, as they value precision and analytical thinking.

Understanding your DISC profile reveals why certain situations and behaviors elicit strong emotional responses, enabling more effective emotional regulation.

Question 2: What can I do if I struggle to identify my emotional triggers?

Answer 2: Identifying emotional triggers can be challenging, primarily if you're not used to introspection. Take your time. Consider situations where you've experienced solid emotional responses, and reflect on commonalities between them. Seeking feedback from others helps, giving us an outside perspective on patterns we may not notice.

Question 3: I've identified my emotional triggers. How can I change the way I react to them?

Answer 3: You can try several things, such as conscious breathing techniques, positive self-talk, or momentarily removing yourself from a situation. The goal isn't to eliminate your emotions but to manage them to align with your DISC style and personal values.

Question 4: How does practicing an emotion-management strategy improve my interpersonal relationships?

Answer 4: When you're better able to manage your emotions, you communicate more effectively, make considered decisions, and are less likely to engage in conflict. This leads to positive interactions and a deeper understanding between you and others, improving your personal and professional relationships.

Question 5: How can I use my DISC personality strengths to manage my emotional responses?

Answer 5: By fully understanding them. Each DISC profile has unique strengths you can leverage in emotion management. For example:

- Suppose you're a high Dominance (D) type. In that case, your assertiveness and ability to make quick decisions are beneficial in a crisis, allowing you to take immediate action rather than be overwhelmed by emotions.

- If you're a high Influence (I) type, your optimism and ability to express yourself are helpful with reframing negative situations more positively. Your enthusiasm will also help lift the spirits of those around you.

- If you're a high Steadiness (S) type, patience and stability are beneficial when faced with emotionally charged situations. There's a good chance that you find it easy to stay calm and composed, allowing you to react more thoughtfully.

- If you're a high Conscientiousness (C) type, your analytical and careful nature help you stay composed under pressure. You're likely to think before reacting, which prevents emotional escalation.

17. Fostering Constructive Feedback

Purpose: The goal with this activity is to learn how to better use DISC styles to encourage and engage feedback. Break into small clusters and engage in meaningful discourse regarding effective ways to exchange feedback tailored to your distinct DISC personality types.

Instructions:

1. Divide your team into partners and designate roles: one delivers feedback and the other acts as recipient.

2. Now it's time for self-assessment. Give everyone a blank canvas in the form of a sheet of paper. Encourage them to embark on a path of self-discovery, reflecting on their inherent strengths and weaknesses through the lens of their DISC profiles.

3. They share thoughtful feedback with their partner, centered around their self-assessed strengths and weaknesses. Focus should be on the way they communicate and collaborate with others.

4. Active listening is imperative. The receiver's role is to absorb feedback with an open mind, actively listening and taking salient points to heart.

5. Then reverse roles and repeat the process, allowing both partners to experience the nuances of giving and receiving feedback.

6. End with a group debriefing session. As a unified team, engage in a lively discussion about the exercise and reflect on the insights gained.

Big Idea: This exercise assists team members in understanding and effectively using their DISC strengths and weaknesses to exchange feedback.

Outcome: Participants will gain a refined understanding of imparting and receiving feedback congruent with their DISC profile—helping improve communication skills and paving the way for personal growth and synergistic team interaction.

Team Q&A: Below are five potential questions a facilitator might expect to encounter while conducting this exercise, along with helpful answers for each:

Question 1: How does my DISC profile influence my giving and receiving feedback?

Answer 1: Your profile reflects your behavioral style, which shapes your feedback style. For instance:

- A high Dominance (D) profile might provide feedback directly and assertively, expecting others to be straightforward and decisive.

- A high Influence (I) profile may give and receive feedback in an enthusiastic, positive manner, often focusing on interpersonal relationships and the broader picture rather than the nitty-gritty details.

- A high Steadiness (S) profile might deliver feedback in a gentler, diplomatic way, valuing harmony and constructive and supportive feedback.

- A high Conscientiousness (C) profile might offer detailed, analytical feedback on accuracy and quality. They likely appreciate precise, well-considered observations over general comments.

Recognizing these tendencies helps you adapt your feedback style when interacting with different DISC profiles.

Question 2: What should I focus on when giving feedback to my partner?

Answer 2: Keep your feedback constructive and relevant as you focus on your partner's self-assessed strengths and weaknesses. Keep their DISC profile in mind. Your goal is to help your partner grow and improve. Be sure to deliver your feedback in an actionable, respectful, and considerate manner.

Question 3: I find it difficult to accept feedback. How can I improve on this?

Answer 3: It's common to feel defensive when receiving feedback, but we must keep our eyes on the prize: Feedback is a valuable tool for our growth, so try to view it as an opportunity to learn and improve. Practice active listening, avoid getting defensive, and ask for clarification if you don't understand something. Understanding your DISC profile also helps. Knowing how you prefer to receive feedback makes it easier to describe your style to others and ensures a more comfortable process.

Question 4: How can I provide feedback to someone whose DISC profile differs from mine?

Answer 4: Tailor your feedback specifically to the recipient's style. For example:

- If you're a high Dominance (D) style communicating with a high Conscientiousness (C) style, be detailed and systematic in your feedback. Emphasize concrete facts and specific examples.

- Conversely, if you're a high Influence (I) style communicating with a high Steadiness (S) style, be gentle and supportive with your feedback. Focus on the person's effort and areas for improvement.

With an understanding of DISC profiles, you adjust your feedback to ensure it's well received.

Question 5: We've completed the exercise. How can we apply what we've learned about giving and receiving feedback to our everyday work lives?

Answer 5: You understand your DISC profile better, including how it impacts your feedback style—and you use this knowledge to navigate future feedback exchanges, whether you're reviewing a colleague's work or receiving comments regarding your performance. This increased awareness and adaptability improves communication and strengthens team relationships.

18. Strategizing Time Management

Purpose: The goal with this exercise is all about tailoring DISC styles to time management. Participants will form compact groups to discuss time-management techniques harmonized with personality types based on the DISC model.

Instructions:

1. Have each team member take the DISC assessment to help identify dominant behavioral styles.

2. Provide participants with a time-management inventory (a time audit). This tool gauges existing habits and patterns in time management.

3. Next, break participants into small groups for deliberation. Ask them to scrutinize the disparate DISC-compatible time-management methods. Explore why a D type might gravitate toward a regimented, orderly schedule, while an I type might revel in a more flexible timeline, generously punctuated with social interactions and spontaneity. Consider the various time-management approaches as they relate to DISC profiles. What do participants see as key strengths and potential challenges?

4. Participants will now turn their attention inward, reflecting on innate time and management tendencies and mulling over ways to tweak their style for heightened efficiency.

5. With these insights, they should craft a personalized action plan, jotting down tangible steps to hone time-management skills by drawing from their DISC profile. For example, an S type may wish to set concrete deadlines and reminders to remain on course and meet objectives.

6. Now it's time to set their plan in motion through evaluation, closely monitoring their progress and finetuning strategy based on experiences.

Big Idea: This exercise is a bridge to understanding someone's inherent approach to time management, helping formulate strategies suited to their DISC profile.

Outcome: Participants are armed with time-management techniques tailored to their personality, and they embrace these personalized strategies to amplify productivity.

Team Q&A: Below are five potential questions a facilitator might expect to encounter while conducting this exercise, along with helpful answers for each:

Question 1: How does my DISC profile influence my time-management habits?

Answer 1: Each DISC style has different preferences and approaches. For instance:

- If you're a high Dominance (D) individual, you might prefer a structured schedule with clear goals and deadlines. Efficiency and control may be high priorities for you.

- If you're high in Influence (I), you might enjoy a more flexible schedule with ample room for social interaction. It's likely that you draw energy from dynamic environments and prefer variety.

- If you're high in Steadiness (S), you may favor a consistent, predictable schedule, with plenty of time dedicated to supporting others and maintaining harmony within your work environment.

- If you're high in Conscientiousness (C), you might appreciate a well-organized and detailed plan focusing on accuracy and quality. You may prefer to work methodically, dedicating time to ensuring precision.

Understanding your profile helps you tailor your time-management strategies for maximum productivity and satisfaction, playing to your strengths and mitigating weaknesses.

Question 2: What's the purpose of time auditing in this exercise?

Answer 2: It's crucial in understanding your time-management habits. By evaluating how you spend your time and identifying patterns, you gain insight into what works, including areas for improvement. This provides a baseline for a personalized time-management strategy that aligns with your DISC profile.

Question 3: I'm a C type and tend to procrastinate. How can I overcome this?

Answer 3: As a Conscientiousness style, you might find yourself bogged down in a pursuit for perfection, which may lead to procrastination. In this case (and in all cases), set specific deadlines for tasks and break them down into manageable steps. You can overcome procrastination by reaching progressive milestones rather than striving for being perfect. It's about progress over perfection.

Question 4: How can I tailor my time-management strategies based on my DISC profile?

Answer 4: You leverage the strengths of your DISC profile while managing potential challenges. Each style features different strengths and potential areas for improvement. For example:

- If you're a Steadiness (S) type, you might benefit from concrete deadlines and reminders to ensure that you complete tasks on time. You could also use your natural ability to create a harmonious work environment to foster teamwork and shared responsibility.

- If you're a Dominance (D) style, try incorporating flexibility into your schedule to allow unexpected tasks and changes. Practicing patience and understanding when dealing with team members who work at a different pace enhances collaboration.

- If you're high in Influence (I), sociability and enthusiasm are excellent for boosting team morale. Just make sure that they don't distract from the tasks at hand. Use tools to help organize your time and keep track of deadlines.

- If you're high in Conscientiousness (C), your attention to detail is a strength, but it could land you in the weeds. Strike a balance between your need for precision and the necessity of meeting deadlines.

Awareness of your DISC style helps you maximize productivity and maintain a satisfying work-life balance.

Question 5: How can I evaluate the effectiveness of my new time-management strategy?

Answer 5: Evaluation is a critical part of the process. As you implement your new strategy, monitor your progress regularly. Pay attention to how you feel: Are you more productive? Have your stress levels decreased? Consider how well you're meeting deadlines and achieving goals. Strategically tweak your strategy based on your observations. Effective time management is a continuous process requiring lots of adaptation.

19. Guided Development (Mentors)

Purpose: The aim with this activity is to gain a deeper understanding of a DISC style with a mentor's help. In intimate groups, participants try their hand at mentoring one another, tailoring guidance per each other's personality styles.

Instructions:

1. First, select a mentor who's well-versed in the DISC framework. Think about your colleagues and superiors. Can someone with a solid grasp of the framework provide constructive feedback?

2. Then turn the lens inward and identify the areas you aspire to enhance in your own style. For instance, if you lean toward a Dominance (D) style, you might hone your communication skills to bolster deeper bonds with colleagues. Based on your DISC profile, can you identify any aspects you'd like to improve?

3. Now, you formulate a strategy. Both mentor and mentee should devise a plan together based on skill development. Create specific objectives and a sequence of actionable steps to guide the mentee toward their targets.

4. Next, practice the skills you've targeted for improvement. Along this journey, your mentor will be your guiding star, offering feedback and direction.

5. Finally, evaluate your progress. Conduct routine evaluations to monitor headway and make adjustments, ensuring that your strategy remains relevant and practical.

Big Idea: This exercise aims to accelerate personal and professional growth. Individuals can pinpoint their strengths and weaknesses, as well as enhance their abilities, with the sympathetic aid of a mentor.

Outcome: Participants improve their targeted skills and gain deeper self-awareness. Guided by a mentor, they receive insightful feedback and support that empowers them to reach their full potential as influential leaders and invaluable team players.

Team Q&A: Below are five potential questions a facilitator might expect to encounter while conducting this exercise, along with helpful answers for each:

Question 1: How important is the mentor's understanding of the DISC framework?

Answer 1: It's crucial. The DISC model is the guiding structure of this coaching process. A solid understanding of the four DISC styles—Dominance, Influence, Steadiness, and Conscientiousness—allows the mentor to better understand the mentee's communication style, work preferences, motivations, and potential weaknesses. This enables the mentor to provide tailored, practical guidance that aligns with the mentee's personality and needs.

Question 2: How do we identify aspects of ourselves that we might want to improve based on our DISC profile?

Answer 2: Your DISC profile provides valuable insight into your strengths and potential weaknesses. For instance, if your style leans heavily toward Dominance (D), although you may be excellent at taking initiative and making quick decisions, you might need help with patience and empathy while communicating. These insights help you identify skills for development, such as improving your ability to communicate effectively with colleagues with different DISC styles.

Question 3: What objectives and actionable steps should we include in our strategy?

Answer 3: Objectives should be specific, measurable, attainable, relevant, and time-bound (SMART). For example, suppose your goal is to improve your communication skills. An objective might be: "Effectively communicate project expectations to my team, reducing clarifying questions by 50% over the next three months." Actionable steps could include attending a communication workshop, practicing active listening, or scheduling regular feedback sessions with your team.

Question 4: How does this coaching process foster personal growth?

Answer 4: Not only does this coaching process help you improve specific skills but it also fosters self-awareness. By examining your DISC profile and identifying areas for improvement, you gain a deeper understanding of your behaviors, strengths, and weaknesses. Your mentor provides you with thoughtful third-party feedback and guidance, helping you develop new strategies for personal and professional success.

Question 5: What role does the mentor play in evaluating progress?

Answer 5: Their feedback helps identify areas for further improvement and assists in adjusting strategy as necessary. Their outside perspective and expertise are invaluable in helping you gauge your progress and navigate challenges that arise along the way. The mentor-mentee relationship is dynamic—open communication and mutual respect are crucial to success.

20. Mastering the Art of Delegation

Purpose: The objective with this exercise centers around learning to delegate according to DISC styles. In small groups, participants explore the art of delegation, creating strategies for delegating tasks depending on their distinct personality types.

Instructions:

1. Make sure that each participant has taken a DISC assessment.

2. Begin by clarifying and emphasizing the vital role that delegation plays in leadership and team management. Why do you think delegation is crucial for effective leadership?

3. Next, split the group into pairs. Have each participant reveal their DISC-determined delegation style and compare it with their partner's. How does their delegation style differ from their partner's, based on the DISC profiles?

4. Encourage pairs to discuss their strengths and weaknesses concerning delegation. Have them provide constructive feedback regarding each other's potential areas for improvement.

5. Once the pairs have had a rich discussion, reconvene and share insights. Request that volunteers share their newfound wisdom and strategies for finetuning their delegation style to better suit various team members.

6. Finally, have a group discussion. Facilitate a group dialogue that covers the best practices for effective delegation. Touch on the delicate balance between trust and control, the importance of communicating expectations, and providing continuous support and feedback to team members.

Big Idea: This activity aims to help team members understand their delegation style and equip them with practical strategies for adapting their style to suit other members' needs.

Outcome: Participants expand their self-awareness concerning their delegation style, elevating their leadership capabilities and enhancing proficiency in team management. Ultimately, it fuels an environment of mutual growth and performance.

Team Q&A: Below are five potential questions a facilitator might expect to encounter while conducting this exercise, along with helpful answers for each:

Question 1: Why is delegation considered a crucial aspect of effective leadership?

Answer 1: It allows leaders to distribute work efficiently, promoting team engagement and productivity. By assigning tasks to team members, leaders demonstrate trust and confidence in their team's abilities. This maximizes morale and encourages personal and professional growth, allowing leaders to focus on high-priority tasks and strategic planning.

Question 2: How does the DISC assessment reveal our delegation styles?

Answer 2: The DISC assessment identifies your dominant behavioral traits, including how you typically respond to tasks and challenges and interact with others. This sheds light on your preferred delegation style.

- For instance, those with a Dominance (D) trait may delegate tasks assertively and expect quick results. They tend to set clear goals and expect team members to meet them.

- Individuals with an Influence (I) trait might delegate tasks more collaboratively and enthusiastically, focusing on creating an engaging and fun environment. They often rely on their interpersonal relationships and persuasive skills when delegating tasks.

- People with a high Steadiness (S) trait are often patient and supportive, delegating tasks in a more consultative manner. They usually greatly emphasize harmony, ensuring that everyone is comfortable with their assigned tasks.

- Those with a Conscientiousness (C) trait might delegate tasks meticulously, giving precise instructions and expecting thoroughness in return. They likely double-check tasks before delegating them to ensure accuracy, often preferring a systematic and organized approach to task management.

By understanding your delegation style, you more effectively lead teams and adapt your approach as required, depending on individuals and situations.

Question 3: How do our DISC profiles affect our delegation styles?

Answer 3: Your profile is a comprehensive assessment of your personal traits—including how you communicate—and delegation is a vital aspect of strategic communication. Each profile has its unique approach and challenges related to delegation. For example:

- A leader with a Dominance (D) profile might delegate tasks quickly and decisively. They tend to focus on end goals and expect rapid results. Therefore, they need to focus on providing clear instructions while ensuring that they allow enough autonomy for their team to thrive.

- A leader with an Influence (I) profile likely uses their interpersonal skills to delegate, aiming to inspire and motivate teams. Although they're known for creating an enthusiastic and collaborative work environment, they must pay more attention to details and ensure that tasks are completed on time.

- A leader with a Steadiness (S) profile usually prefers a supportive and patient delegation approach. They tend to care about the feelings and comfort of team members, and they may ensure consultation when delegating tasks. However, they might need to work on pushing their team out of their comfort zones for growth and development.

- A leader with a Conscientiousness (C) profile might provide detailed instructions and expect tasks to be done accurately and thoroughly. They value high standards and a systematic approach. While these qualities ensure high output, they may need to work on trusting their team's capabilities and not micromanaging.

Understanding your delegation style according to your DISC profile helps you refine your leadership approach, leading to increased team effectiveness and productivity.

Question 4: How can we effectively discuss our strengths and weaknesses in delegation?

Answer 4: It's essential to approach the conversation with openness and respect. Start by reflecting on your experiences and observations regarding your delegation style, and then listen actively when your partner shares their feedback. The goal isn't to critique but to understand and improve your delegation practices.

Question 5: What are some best practices for effective delegation?

Answer 5: They include communicating tasks and expected outcomes, ensuring that an individual has the necessary resources and skills, and assigning responsibility and authority proportionately. Set a realistic timeline and offer support and feedback. Make sure that you're recognizing and appreciating effort and good work. The goal of delegation isn't simply to distribute tasks but to empower team members and contribute to their professional development.

About the Author

Dr. Christopher P. Meade holds a PhD in Adult & Organizational Learning with a concentration in leadership. He also holds two master's degrees and a certificate in Disruptive Strategy from Harvard Business School. As a former business school dean and acclaimed graduate instructor, Christopher has coached and trained over 25,000 leaders and facilitated team training for numerous Fortune 500 organizations. Christopher speaks at leadership events and team training events throughout the United States. He is the author of multiple books on leadership and personal and professional development, including *Leadership Alive: Changing Leadership Practices in the Emerging 21st Century Culture; Leading Strategic Change, Innovation & Transformation: The 10 Elements of Successful Change Leadership; Team Accelerators: The Seven Force Multipliers of High-Performance Teams; Servantology: The Periodic Elements of Servant Leadership; Emotional Intelligence: Another Kind of Smart; Trust Accelerators: Activating the Domino Effect That Accelerates Team Engagement, Innovation, and High-Performance;* and *Trusted Servant Leadership: A New Kind of Leader for a New Kind of World.*

> I want to inspire leaders to be extraordinary. Everything I do is designed to catalyze growth in others and propel them toward a better version of themselves so that they can more meaningfully touch the lives of others in the work they do each day.

—Christopher P. Meade, PhD

www.ingramcontent.com/pod-product-compliance
Lightning Source LLC
Chambersburg PA
CBHW021539150726
47990CB00006B/2310